The Song and the Silence

*For my Stoney Indian friends and
Canada's original people
everywhere*

The Song and the Silence
Sitting Wind

The Life of Stoney Indian Chief
Frank Kaquitts

PETER JONKER

LONE
PINE

The Publishers:
Lone Pine Publishing
206, 10426-81 Avenue
Edmonton, Alberta
T6E 1X5

Canadian Cataloguing in Publication Data
Jonker, Peter Marinus, 1946-
  Sitting Wind

  ISBN 0-919433-54-5

  1. Kaquitts, Frank, 1925- 2.Assiniboin Indians -
Biography. 3. Assiniboin Indians - History. 4. Indians of
North America - Alberta - Biography. 5. Indians of North
America - Alberta - History. I. Title.
E99.A84K36 1988 971.23'00497 C88-091465-3

Cover photo - Peter M. Jonker
Cover design - Yuet C. Chan
Editorial - Mary Walters Riskin
Printing - Quebecor Jasper Printing

Publisher's Acknowledgement
The publisher gratefully acknowledges the assistance of
the Federal Department of Communication, Alberta
Culture, the Canada Council, and the Alberta Foundation
for the Literary Arts in the production of this book.

Foreword

It is my view that a fact becomes mostly fiction at the very moment of its being observed. And, with that preamble, it must be impressed upon the reader that the events described within the following pages are fact in that they actually occurred. However, insofar as these same events were once recorded by Sitting Wind's eyes and ears (and some by mine as well), they must equally be considered fiction.

This book cannot therefore be dubbed a documentary. Nor is it a novel. It is closer to some blend of these two: "docu-fiction," perhaps, or "a true romantic tale".

From the book's inception, my purpose in committing to paper this series of vignettes describing moments in Sitting Wind's life was not merely to present for the record a series of events. The events in themselves are rather ordinary, almost trivial, and could have occurred (and probably did) in the lives of many other Canadian Indians. What I intended was to make it possible for each reader to develop new awareness of the depth at which values are embedded within a culture, and the painful disorientation generated at intersections where cultural values clash.

More than stubborn optimism is often required of a minority group member to withstand such clashes. Sitting Wind has managed to survive intact. I have known others whose inner resources were less than the demands made upon them.

Peter Jonker, 1988

Acknowledgements

Many people have contributed to the process of writing this book, some directly, others indirectly. I thank them all. I am deeply indebted to Jon Whyte, whose direction and excellent critiques were fundamental. Thanks to Bob Sandford for his observations and encouragement; also to Dr. Hugh Dempsey and Eileen Smith for their valuable comments on the draft manuscript. Thanks to my wonderful children Amanda, Daphne, and Garland, for tolerating my self-imposed long hours incommunicado.

Most of all I thank Sitting Wind for his wonderful stories, his genuine honesty, and his unwavering friendship.

Introduction

I think many Canadians, if not most, have no understanding of what an Indian such as myself has to go through during a single lifetime.

Since my days began, more than half a century ago, I have personally experienced great changes. The day I walked into the residential school wearing a breechcloth and leggings, was the day I made my very first steps into the modern world. And my parents were not there to hold my hand and lead me on a familiar path; equipped only with knowledge of bush survival, my guardian could do no more than push me across the doorstep and hope for the best. I was left to survive on my own.

After the author, Peter Jonker, and I had worked together for a couple of years, I as chief and he as my administrator, he offered to write about my past. I was honoured. I saw in this an opportunity to show outsiders first hand what it is like to be an Indian, born on a reserve and trying to cope in today's world.

I hope that every reader becomes more sympathetic and less judgmental of us Indians. We have suffered, and continue to suffer. It is as if we are trying to climb a falling tree. A fallen tree. A strong one which my ancestors grew up with and completely trusted for centuries.

Frank Kaquitts
Morley, Alberta
September, 1988

Contents

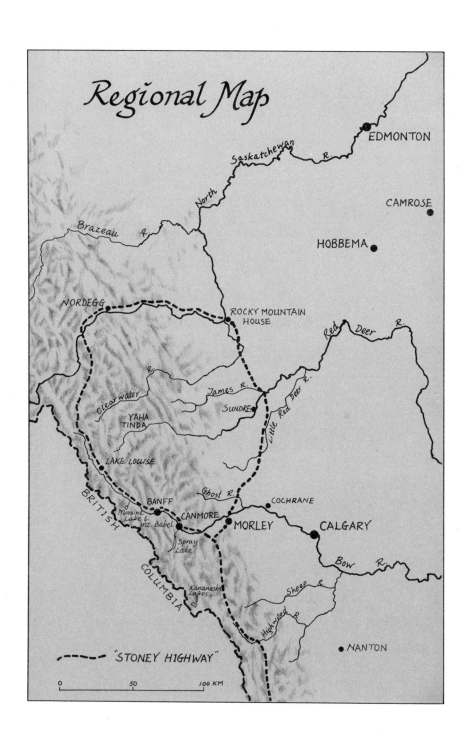

Regional Map

EDMONTON

CAMROSE

HOBBEMA

Saskatchewan R.

North

Brazeau R.

NORDEGG

ROCKY MOUNTAIN
HOUSE

Red *Deer* R.

Clearwater R.

James R.

SUNDRE

Little Red Deer R.

YAHA
TINDA

LAKE LOUISE

BANFF

Ghost R.

COCHRANE

Moraine
Lake &
Mt. Babel

CANMORE

MORLEY

CALGARY

BRITISH

*Spray
Lake*

COLUMBIA

*Kananaskis
Lakes*

Bow R.

Sheep R.

Highwood R.

NANTON

- - - - - "STONEY HIGHWAY"

0   50   100 KM

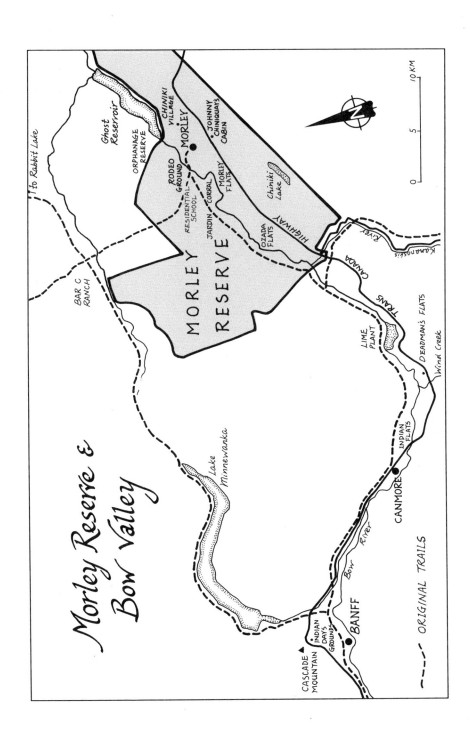

Morley Reserve & Bow Valley

to Rabbit Lake

Ghost Reservoir

ORPHANAGE RESERVE

CHINIKI VILLAGE

MORLEY

JOHNNY CHINIQUAY'S CABIN

RODEO GROUND

RESIDENTIAL SCHOOL

JARDIN CORRAL

MORLEY FLATS

Chiniki Lake

MORLEY RESERVE

OZADA FLATS

HIGHWAY

BAR C RANCH

Kananaskis River

TRANS CANADA

LIME PLANT

DEADMAN'S FLATS

Wind Creek

Lake Minnewanka

INDIAN FLATS

CANMORE

Bow River

CASCADE MOUNTAIN

INDIAN DAY'S GROUNDS

BANFF

ORIGINAL TRAILS

N

10 KM

5

0

Hobbema Indian Reserve
February, 1926

Footsteps crunching outside the door are unmistakable this time. Mary quickly wraps the weakened baby lying in her lap, and the cabin door opens as John and Norman — her husband and their oldest son — enter in a veil of ice fog.

"You'd better call the medicine man right away."

Although her voice is controlled and soliciting, Mary's eyes reveal her panic.

John sets an armful of frozen, snow-dusted wood into a corner behind the tin stove, and 16-year-old Norman follows with his. No further words are exchanged: there is no choice.

The Indian mother is seated on a moose-hide floor-covering in the same dingy cabin where she gave birth to the baby, about a year ago. She cannot recall exactly when he was born, but Snow's Middle Season was giving way to the Rooyah Tahway, or Moon Month. The cycle of one year's passing has brought back the same cold moon. But how different are the circumstances, with the infant now hovering near death.

The blizzard outside has muddled Mary's perception of time. It must be well into the afternoon, or perhaps later. The snow started as a controlled and gentle fall before first light, but rapidly and viciously disintegrated, temperatures plummeting throughout the morning. Tiny flakes have frozen into brittle sharp needles which will scour exposed skin.

While she cradles the baby, weakly now, snow gusts surge angrily outside, whispering and shifting like evil spirits along the exterior walls, seeking icy entry through cracks between the logs. A conspiracy of forces she cannot fathom is plunging her child toward some irreversible fate. His death appears imminent: just a matter of time. She pulls him closer into the semi-circle of her lap.

As he leaves to find the healer, she sees John's eyes briefly probe the cabin's dark interior where the remaining children have retreated to their bedding again, apparently behaved.

He has provided well for the six of them: eight, including himself and her. In spite of the demands made upon him by a family of this size, he has successfully accumulated the tools and the horses required for reasonable comfort. Next fall, he says, he will buy a buckboard and harness if he finds enough work with local ranchers. The medicine man will have to be paid of course, but he can afford the sacrifice.

The door closes behind them. Alone again in her watch, Mary feels the chill circulate inside the cabin. It slides across her neck, like a predator feigning attack, testing her resistance, looking for points of entry through her defences. Testing her child's fading strength as well. The wait for the medicine man will be difficult, and long.

Earlier in the day the five older children awoke and romped for a while, but soon all of them except her first-born returned to their fur covers which are spread in a sweaty tangle around the stove. Only their grandma's bundled form against the wall has remained motionless, in complete acceptance of the vicissitudes of nature.

There is not enough space in the cabin for playing. It is a sleeping place only: a single room featuring a scantily-covered dirt floor. A den like a bear's, large enough only to fit the family tight to the walls. There's nothing for its occupants to do on a day such as this, but wait.

Mary recalls seeing large houses belonging to whitemen — only a couple of children, and many rooms. At Rocky Mountain House, she has seen windows containing glass. Here in their Indian shack, nearly swallowed by the rolling bushland, an empty flour sack — stretched in the south-facing window hole — is flapping in the wind, snow eddies curling around loose fringes. She tries to imagine her cabin's window with real glass.

Cabins are warmer in winter, John tells her; even with a poor window and faulty chinking. He built this one using poplar logs cut on the bench above the river. A generation ago, there were only tepees: the original ones, constructed of tanned deer hides. They kept out the wind, and the fire within kept them snug. But the deer became scarce when whitemen increased in numbers, and the hides were hard to obtain. Thereafter, the Trading Post canvas became tepee coverings, and they were good for summer only. Tepees are becoming, more and more, a summer travelling lodge.

Her eyes shift from the window to the ceiling.

John Morin is capable; he takes charge. He is a strong and stubborn man. He laid split logs flat over the walls and covered the cracks with bark. A heavy layer of dirt thrown over the bark holds in heat from the tin stove. She imagines the pale dry grass culms, sprung from the roof, all arched away from the distant mountains in a glorious tangle. The cold makes them brittle. The snow whips around them, and buries them.

Feelings of love, renewed during the Christmas and New Year's feasting with John's Cree clan on the Hobbema reserve, surface easily, to linger like warm embers in Mary's thoughts. Usually, she cannot resist fondling them like amulets against these most bitter days of the seasonal cycle. But today this is impossible. Christmas was six weeks ago. During the snow season, six weeks can bring hunger and desperate cold. Can bring death.

Such a handsome baby. Her raw cold lips, pressing his cheeks, arouse a maimed startle response. She croons an apology of sound, for the child's tender skin is flushed with searing fever. She thinks of her own fevers long ago, the delirium: falling out of a tree and never hitting ground, the ground falling away into a void, running from a cougar's outstretched claws but never fast enough. The overwhelming helplessness of having to run forever, unable to escape, unable to be free.

All children should be given the chance to grow up healthy and free, she thinks: challenged step by step, by the elements, protected by their guardian Spirits.

Her baby. Frank.

On a balmy day last autumn, she and John took him, along with the older sons, to collect their annual five-dollar-a-head Treaty payment, and the Indian Agent questioned them closely about the time of the baby's birth. He wrote perfect diagonal letters in the register book, pen nib scraping like a junco scratching dead leaves.

"And what is his name?" he asked suddenly.

Time snagged awkwardly: uncertain, suspended. The pen stopped and the agent's hairy upturned face assumed a fatherly expression. The gold cap on his front tooth glinted officiously in the bright sun. The boys chased a ground squirrel behind his makeshift table, involved in a conspiracy of animated whispers about another burrow entrance beside the wagon.

Mary's eyes were riveted to the ground. It was a question that could not be answered.

John spoke, rescuing the moment.

"We didn't give him a name yet."

The agent glanced through the list of first names on the page before him: the oldest brother was Norman, and then there was Joseph, Peter, Edward, and Paul.

"Y'll have to do something about that," he said. "Can't have the little fellow growing up without a proper Christian name.'' He smiled generously as he spoke, and then began to list some other, suitable names.

''Frank?'' Mary glanced sideways at John, echoing one of the names the agent had listed. ''We could call him Frank.''

The agent's pen scratched again, tracing ink across the page like the moist black thread from a spider. This was his business, the business of the Queen. There was no hesitation. It was final. The register said, ''February 28, 1925: Frank Morin''.

The thin logs creak and snap under the storm's siege, jolting her back to the present. Why is it taking so long for John and Norman to find the medicine man? Precious moments are slipping away. Something must be done, now. Before it's too late. But what? What can she do that she has not done already?

Awareness of the precariousness of life floods her with a sense of helplessness. Her baby's continued breath depends on whims, whims that can wipe him out without as much as a last cry, at any moment. No plan can challenge the awesome magic that is burning up her baby. There will be no recourse, no way to avenge the death. Can she do nothing but be silent? Acquiesce to fate?

Cold air begins to seep through gaps between her cradling arms. Mary pulls the ends of the blanket-wrap more closely about the infant in her lap. She tries to resign herself again to the wait: just as her mother, Moraha, sleeping against the wall in a warm blanket curl, seems so peacefully resigned.

Mary's very first child, the boy she had with Moise Katchemook, died before the age of two. It seems long in the past. And she lost a girl baby a couple of summers ago, not long after it was born. Still, six children alive is a remarkable family these days. She is almost thirty, and has lost only two.

When her belly started enlarging once again, with this baby, she hoped it would be another girl. A girl would become an important help for her. There is always work to do, especially since her Cree mother — now only a visitor at Hobbema — married a Stoney Indian and left this reserve to live in Morley. But the Spirits had other plans.

A small, transient smile starts on her lips as she recalls the disappointment that came over her when the infant fell squelching and sputtering into the hands of the medicine woman who told her it was a boy. But even during the pain of the moment, she accepted the divine will. If the Great Spirit chose a boy, she told herself, there must be good reason. Very good reason. This boy must have a special destiny.

A frown crowds her forehead. Does the Great Spirit remain in control at all times, without sleeping or looking away? Can she depend on Him? Her ears search through the cacophony braided into the storm, listening for a sound that may be help approaching. Does the Almighty God change His mind sometimes? The thought troubles her. If only one could be certain.

The missionaries taught them about Almighty God. Her grandfather told her about the coming of the missionaries. A few had ventured far westward up the North Saskatchewan basin into Canada's interior, paddling canoes, winding across the expanses of prairie and aspen and boreal forests between trading posts at Fort Garry (Winnipeg) and Edmonton House. They penetrated the heart of Cree country.

The man whom the Stoneys remember as "Black Head" was the first. The whitemen called him Robert Rundle. A dedicated Christian, he not only learned to speak Cree, but also translated the Bible into Cree and translated the hymns so Indians could sing to the Christian God in their native tongue. Later, George and John McDougall worked among the Stoneys at Morley, and encouraged them to sing Cree songs. Mary does not believe those people who suggest, cynically, that missionaries were promoted by a fur-company to bring peace among the tribes, so Indians could be enticed to trap furs instead of fighting.

When she was young, she often went to church at Morley to hear John McDougall's speeches. "There is only one God in all the world," his voice would thunder from the stand. "He is the Almighty Ruler of the universe, the same for all people whether white or Indian or any other race! Pray to him and read His Holy Word, and you will be saved from the terror of burning forever in the fiery lake!" His face gleamed with sweat, and his arms swept the air above and before him as if he were fighting a courageous battle with the devil spirit right there for everyone to see.

She felt small and helpless at church: who would dare to disagree, even in her thoughts, with such powerful words? Mary does not like to feel helpless. But she also found a comfort there, in a ruling God more powerful than this fever, than this storm. More powerful than anything.

Rocking little Frank in her lap, Mary softly hums "Amazing Grace" in flat, lilting tones.

John Morin first became acquainted with her when she was living with Katchemook. He never took to Katchemook because, he confided to her one night when her head rested on his shoulder under the bedding furs, he was "two-faced like a wolverine".

He was right. Katchemook used to beat her for no reason. She remembers his fist approaching, blood-stained from skinning beavers. Chills prickle her neck at the memory of those first few years away from her parents. The loneliness. The helplessness. When their child died and Mary's father died in the same summer, Katchemook flew into a demonic rage and sent her away.

"I want my children to be a nest of strong hunters," he raved. "Fighters who will be great. Children who will bring honour! Do you think the addition of a worn-out mother-in-law will satisfy me?"

John made her feel attractive and capable. He was a good hunter, and he wasn't afraid of Katchemook, either.

They talked sometimes when no one was around to mock them, or to raise gossip about them. He informed his father, and their parents discussed the matter. Of course Mary's Cree mother, Moraha La-zyback, agreed immediately: as long as she could stay with them. Since her first Stoney husband had died, she'd been worried about who would take care of them.

It was settled. Mary left the Stoney Indian reserve where she was raised and moved in with John at Hobbema, where everyone was a stranger. It was good that her mother spent those first few years with her. Moraha knew people at Hobbema, and for Mary she was someone familiar to talk to.

John has been a good provider. Fearless of anything — like the legendary Stoney, Crooked Neck, who never flinched when he was outnumbered in battle, like the current respected leader and medicine man, Hector Crawler. Other women make comments to one another about John; she has overheard them sometimes. She knows that they are jealous.

Thanks to John, food is never scarce, and they are sheltered. Her eyes lift to the storage shelf in the corner. Slabs of dry-meat have reshaped one of the sacks which rest on it: rugged pinnacles stab outward. It is an old flour sack. The circular label stamped on the densely woven cloth is still legible: Gold Seal. The other bags contain flour, tea, and sugar.

Moraha stayed with them several years before she met her new Stoney husband, Ben Kaquitts. She was an invaluable companion and teacher, helping Mary to raise the children, scrape the hides, dig roots, and prepare the meat. Mary's success is proven now. She has John's complete confidence.

Perhaps he has never doubted her ability from the beginning; maybe it is she herself who has gained confidence in her homemaking abilities. But she doesn't want that confidence to change. It must not be called into question, be reconsidered. As long as she's been with John, only one child has died.

It has been more strenuous since Moraha moved back to Morley, especially at first. The days have been too long, and there is so much work to keep up with hunting and the children.

On one hand, it will be good when her boys begin hunting game for food. People will hear about it and talk. More relatives and neighbours will come in from even greater distances to benefit from the success of her man and her children. But it will also mean an increase in women's chores.

The boys will take up with girls, of course. Of course they will take up with girls: they will have to. That's how they will bring helpers into the family.

She looks across at the sleeping forms of her other children. She tries to imagine twelve-year-old Pete sleeping with Sarah Ravenbeak: giggling, touching her small breasts. She saw them talking at the Christmas feast, their chins greased with pemmican.

The sharp butt of a willow is jabbing her through the moose hide spread over the dirt floor, and she shifts her bulk. Baby Frank refuses to suckle her breast in spite of her urging; his moans have deteriorated into whimpering gasps.

Gently, she pushes a hand down the front of his snugly wrapped blanket. The moss is still dry, but the skin is afire. Lovingly, she strokes back the black hair on his burning forehead.

Last year, in preparation for the delivery of this baby, she went on several moss collecting excursions during the Wasahsa Wahien-yahba, the Flower Blooming season, leaving the little boys to look after Paul.

She remembers the sensations: the sun burning on her exposed arms; the musty smell of soil shaken from fresh clumps; the sweet thick taste of vagabond rose-hips; wads of spongy moss spread to dry on prickly spruce boughs.

Later, when the moss was dry, she returned to collect it: sacks full, for the baby's moss bag, to keep him dry and clean. She observed a squirrel tucking meaty cinnamon mushrooms into crevices between branches. Grandfather once told her how the squirrel had taught people this trick. The squirrel is a friend. The mushrooms are strong medicine.

She pictures the squirrel in its nest, a miniscule bit of lonely life in some spruce tree, besieged by winds that take in thousands of miles of forest and mountains in a single day's sweep. There the squirrel clings, a tight curl of tenuous warmth in a core of soft grasses wrapped in a larger globe of sticks and twigs, swaying uncertainly.

Before the snow season arrived and the family settled back into the cabin for the winter, she led the children down to the willows near the river. Taught them how to cut heaps of fresh boughs, and then helped carry them back. All the old, rotting willows were scraped up from the cabin floor, and the fresh ones laid down smoothly, their sweet aroma lasting for many days. It is warmer and drier with willows under the floor hides. She enjoys the feeling of the cabin's being clean.

"John?"

She has turned her head toward the door, believing for a moment she has heard the crunch of his returning footsteps. There is no response, other than wind slapping and sighing. Grainy flakes are being pushed through the door-boards, building tiny drifts immediately inside the cracks. A person could get lost in a blizzard like this one.

John has always shown extra care and alertness during her pregnancies and deliveries. She recalls informing him one day last year that the new baby would be born now, that it was time to call the others. He knew exactly what to do.

The weather was more mellow last winter. He gathered the children and escorted them to his brother's cabin. Then, by horse, he hurried to Beaver Woman's tepee and notified her. Within a couple of hours several women, including the medicine woman, were sitting with Mary. John stayed with the children.

Beaver Woman's medicine was the best available for birthing; other women agreed that she could be trusted. The elder pushed her hand firmly on Mary's stomach. The baby had shifted low. She shuffled outside and suspended the sooty chipped enamel pot from a tripod over the fire and added dry branches to bring up the flames. Undulations of her chants drifted into the cabin, and there were sounds of fumbling by the cooking fire while she prepared a birthing brew. Her chant called upon the Spirits to release their power into the brew, and help Mary have an easy birth. The reassurance was welcome, and the medicine was powerful.

Frank entered the world with not too much pain. Beaver Woman tied off the cord with a length of sinew, cinching it tight, close to the baby's belly, and cutting the cord free.

"He is a boy," Beaver Woman said. "An unusually small one." She sponged with dry moss, deft strokes up and down slimy walnut skin. "But he looks like a tough one, a fighter!"

How he'd protested. A wad of moss was placed between his thrashing legs and he was wrapped into his moss bag. The afterbirth was taken outdoors and buried. Mary rested for a while before she nursed him.

Now, at last, there are sounds at the door latch as John and Norman return. The Medicine Man is with them: Old Mountain Walker, a specialist for children. Mary makes out his faltering, high-pitched voice rising above the tumult of the wind as they approach.

"Someone has angered the snow spirit," he chides. "Maybe we should be walking under thick trees so that we do not step on snow and cause it pain." His laughter is like a snag caught halfway to the ground on a tree: scraping, squeaking. He likes to hear himself. He doesn't care about closing the door quickly.

The medicine bag he brings out from under his blanket is spiritual, made of marten skins with their needle-fanged faces drawn together at the opening, guarding it. Dusty fur around the ears and noses has been rubbed off with age, exposing crusts of cartilage. The hollow eye sockets are dried into blank squints. Mary imagines Old Mountain Walker stirring in his dream sleep, spasms and jerks like a hurt dog, as the Spirits revealed the bag's unique design to him. It is highly personal, and powerful.

Moraha stirs herself into a sitting position. Pete, Ed and Paul crowd in closely with their blankets wrapped around themselves, while Mountain Walker sits down cross-legged before Mary and little Frank.

"Don't come too close."

John's grumble is directed softly at the dusty eager faces fringing the fire light. His words are half-obliterated by a blast of wind, clanging the chimney pipe above the ceiling and bellowing down the vent. The flames within first duff and sizzle under an onslaught of spray, but suddenly respond to fresh oxygen with renewed determination.

Mountain Walker studies the baby intently while all remain mute, respectful of the power of healing Spirits to reverse dire consequences: to do what seems impossible.

As he studies he begins to chant, softly at first, but gradually gaining dominance over the howling elements outside, the sound hovering over the child like a smoke flap in the wind. The marten faces yawn as he opens the bag, exposing his secret store of powerful roots and herbs. He chants over the drink he prepares.

"Feed this to him slowly. A little at a time."

He stands up carefully, his knees pained with arthritis, and promises to return in the early morning for a final treatment.

Several times that night Mary drifts off into welcome slumber, trusting that the healer's medicine has forced the evil spirits into abeyance. But when she wakes to feel the baby lying beside her in the early morning hours, she notices with instant alarm that he is drenched in a death sweat.

The fire is almost cold. It is pitch dark and panic grips her. Her confidence has become as thin as eggshell.

In the cabin's black vacuum she gropes for John's warm body nearby and shakes him urgently.

"You must go right away to bring back Mountain Walker," she whispers hoarsely. "Even though it is dark. Another hour and our baby will be dead."

The helplessness she felt when her girl baby died in infancy has returned in vivid pain. Her hands shake while she enlivens the fire with some small branches and then begins to wipe the infant dry against the cold. John covers himself against the blizzard, and is swallowed up in the night. She tries in vain to nurse the baby once more.

It seems John is gone forever, and Mary is greatly relieved when he materializes with the medicine man back at the cabin door: the two like white-flecked ghosts emerging from a white-out. The old man is wearing a blanket over his shoulders to protect him from the weather. The fire woofs threateningly as the door closes behind them and he nudges the snow from his clothes.

There are no questions. He approaches the baby, waving his fan of feathers over it and chanting, invoking Spirits to work through him.

"I have prayed to my Spirits and they have given me a vision about how your baby shall be cured," he says. "Take him out of the moss bag and lay him on a blanket on this piece of board, naked, with no covers over him."

Mary is dazed with incomplete sleep. Her eyes feel like puffballs about to burst. She thinks she has misunderstood, that she hasn't heard him properly.

"Take him from the moss bag without any covering." His repeat command has icicles in it. The words are unmistakable.

She is astonished that he should make such a request, contradicting all that is safe for such a weakened child. It is too cold to unwrap the baby. The blizzard outside still rages furiously. She longs for Mountain Walker to be friendly and considerate.

She feels strength drain from her fingers; they are like cold brittle branches as she unthreads the thongs and removes the child. Poor child. The mixture of sweat and urine filling her nostrils is suddenly sweet.

She must obey. The command was revealed by Mountain Walker's Spirits.

"Carry him straight outside, into the middle of the wind, but leave the door open," he urges with authority.

Her eyes flit toward John. His discomfort is like a crinkled shirt on his face, and her trust in the healer verges on collapse. But her hesitation is only momentary. How can she possibly protest the instructions? Disobedience would invite unutterable catastrophe. Moraha nods affirmatively from a dim corner, her brown eyes warm, encouraging.

She walks slowly, trembling. The latch is cold iron when she lifts it, and the wind charges in, enveloping her greedily, victoriously. Her instinct is to wrap the blanket around the baby for protection, but those eyes fixed on her back in a colder stare tell her it is forbidden.

Throwing her weight forward, she carries the infant out into the snarling black, the soft orange of the cabin's fire fading as an equal blackness closes in behind her. Only the wailing chant persists, weaving in and out of the blizzard from somewhere behind her, where Mountain Walker stands steadfast in the doorway.

Her moccasins punch holes into the drifts. They are deep. Swish. Swish. Swish. Even as she walks they seem to be reaching up her legs to the thighs with long icy fingers, pulling her down. There's no time to stop, to unhook them, to push them back. She plows on until his muffled voice tells her it is far enough.

Obediently extending her arms, she holds the baby up as an offering to the ravenous cold, to the myriad invisible tiny white fangs attacking. Biting through the blanket, right through her clothes, numbing her flesh. Tearing into her baby's soft body. Her skin is a shell, a frozen rawhide. She wants to run back and huddle by the fire in the stove.

The minutes that pass are like hours, until Mountain Walker's chanting finally diminishes to silence and she hears him calling for her. Pulling the child tightly into her chest, she plunges back. There is more chanting, but the door closes behind her.

When the chanting again ceases completely, the silence within seems larger after battling the tumult outside. The cold from the door, left open for so long, has caused the children to retreat still farther into their furs. The fire spits and roars as John rams in additional fuel. The infant's skin has become as red and fragile as strawberries. He lies very still.

Mountain Walker's face appears like old yellowed snow in the fire light.

"The baby will be cured now. Cover him up."

His gravelly voice speaks more softly, spent. "He will be cured by morning."

He offers Mary more medicine to prepare in a brew, and then swings the blanket like a hood back over his head on the way out, immediately blending with the blizzard once again. The winds almost sweep away his parting words: he will be back again, he says, to complete what the Spirits have revealed.

Mary and John burrow into their blankets and furs, into one another, and eventually fall asleep.

By mid-morning the snowing has stopped. Mary is preparing a stew of rabbit meat and dried saskatoons. The sun has surfaced above the hills, a fuzzy circle trying to push through the shroud of thinning snow clouds.

When, unannounced, Mountain Walker appears in the doorway for the third time, baby Frank is sitting up and playing on the knees of his older brother Pete.

The healer closes the door behind him, explaining to John that the Spirits gave him one more instruction.

"But see! He is healed already!" Mary's relief and excitement glow on her face. "Stay and have some food with us, and join our celebration."

But the elder ignores her and proceeds with his business, waving eagle feathers over the baby's head. Young Pete's eyes grow wide in apprehension of the spiritual leader, towering over him and his baby brother.

The old man begins to sing in his Cree tongue, saying: "You have been healed by the Wind. From now on your name will be Youtnah Peewin, Sitting Wind, because the Wind has healed you. From now on the Wind is your brother. For any illness you may have in the future, call on your brother and he will heal you.

"Sitting Wind! With this name you will be powerful. The Spirits have told me that as long as you call upon the wind, great things are in store for you. You will become a leader of many people. You will live to a ripe old age. Remember your brother. Call him with this special song when you need him, and he will help you."

Mary tries memorize the words, exactly. The lilting song hypnotizes her for the moment.

"A-ai-ai-ai-aa-iii-eeee! A-ai-ai-eeee!"

Frank's personal song for calling his brother, the Wind. The phrase repeats itself again and again in her mind. "This song is to be for this child alone; the leader of many people."

She does not hear the door closing behind Mountain Walker.

Banff
July, 1929

"*Uhn-jeeaboh! Uhn-jeeaboh!* Come and gather! Come and gather! The parade is starting at once!'' Joshua Wildman ambles along a row, from tepee to tepee, cupping his hands to his mouth as he calls. He is the Banff Indian Days camp crier this year, and he takes the role seriously.

Three visitors from Toronto stand courteously to the side in trampled grass, talking and pointing at various Stoney Indians engaged in a hubbub of activities. They single out details of Joshua's bizarre attire. Two black ropes of braided hair fall alongside his ears, a buff and burgundy beaded headband circles his forehead, along with a cap appearing to be made of grizzly fur scraps: long soft filaments shimmering with his movements. A large red-checkered frock covers the clothes of his upper body, and partly spills over a red and black striped Hudson's Bay blanket craftily converted to somewhat baggy, fringed leggings. A wide strap of exquisitely designed bead-work is draped over his shoulder and falls into an ample burgundy and orange bead-work pouch jostling on his hip. At every step a puff of parched dust wafts from beneath his soft-soled moose-hide moccasins.

From within her tepee Moraha hears the crier's voice repeating the message again and again as he proceeds along, each time a little more distant, more absorbed by the larger expanse of the rugged cliffs of Minay Rhappa (Cascade Mountain), which silently overlook the wide meadows containing their camp. Events have lost meaning for her, and her heart cannot find enjoyment in Banff Indian Days festivities this year. The mountain's waterfall continues its descent day after night, and night after day after night, silenced only by periodic winter freeze-up. Time passes similarly for her. It could be yesterday, or last week, or even last year. It does not seem to matter, because Sitting Wind's mother Mary, her only daughter to survive to adulthood, is now also dead: gone to a shadowed resting place where all her other children have gone one by one over the last fifty-nine years of her life. How old she has become, what pitifully little she has to show for all these years slipped by.

When Ben, her Stoney husband, stepped out this morning to ready their horses, a loneliness gripped her again like spasms of deep aching. Like a pleading for help from the far side of a wide and churning river which could never be forded.

Her weary thoughts drift back to her experience of Banff Indian Days in previous years. Last year Mary and John had both been here as well. It was their first visit, in fact: so their boys could spend some time with Grandma. And Mary herself was eager to visit with her mother since Moraha had moved to Morley and they rarely saw each other any more. Their older boys, Pete, Ed, and John, did very well in the foot races and the horse races. Mary tried her luck in the tepee pitching contest while Moraha watched from the periphery, keeping an eye on young Sitting Wind who was prone to waddle off too far, or be overly admired by milling tourists.

Already last year, Moraha muses in retrospect, her daughter was not as strong as she should have been. Of course, she was pregnant again, another baby to follow Sitting Wind; but she was too pale, too tired. She bites her lower lip with a broken row of tarred teeth. If she had only paid more attention to her daughter she could have helped her before it was too late. She remembers everyone laughing, and white people cheering raucously when the poor girl's poles collapsed in a heap onto a wagon as she was frantically trying to wrap the canvas. She thinks of her as a girl because it is her daughter. It was her daughter. They had still given her a prize, even though the poles collapsed. What courage, Moraha reflects, accepting the prize with everyone looking on like that.

She is almost ready now. Seated on a hide inside her tepee, she is half-heartedly tying smoked thongs snugly around her doe skin shin-wraps. After they woke up a few hours ago she made tea to go with some dry-meat. The charred ends of a few branches are still smoldering in the fire circle.

She feels emptiness. Her mind wandering unfocussed, she envisions foxes moving helpless pups to a new den: a mother fox's gleaming white canines gingerly clasping loose neck skin, carrying one like dangling meat to the new place where soil is clean of bugs and lice. It seems to explain why the whitemen keep coming in greater and greater numbers every year: their own lands have become too dirty. It's possibly true. Someone once said the fire-wagon tracks reach farther than any Stoney has ever traveled. Except for one Stoney, that is. William Twin once went to New York, where he said one could travel for two days and yet not escape from cold grey streets, tall flat-faced houses and people flurrying like ants disturbed by the paw of a hungry bear.

The beaded ties for her braids resist her patience. She rewraps the short thong around her braid again still tighter, until finally she is satisfied. Every year in the past she has been able to add some new items to her parade costume. But not this year. This year there seemed to be less time, less energy, less will.

When Mary's child was about to arrive, during the Season of Geese Returning, Moraha travelled from Morley back to Hobbema to help look after John and their boys for a time. Especially the youngest, Sitting Wind.

"Mother." Moraha can still hear the plaintive tone of Mary's voice while they were alone one day stitching hides. "I always feel more tired lately."

Moraha understood and went out to look for new sprouts of mountain spinach (wild sorrel) to help revive her pregnant daughter's strength. She knew where to look for them.

But it was too early. Snow still lay among trees here and there. "When the next moon comes," she assured her, "I will try again and find some for you". Then the baby arrived before the next moon, Mary started bleeding from inside, and no one was able to stop this blood. Beaver Woman had passed on a year earlier. And the other medicine woman, her medicine wasn't strong enough.

"Please stay and help me take care of this baby as long as I am weak."

Of course she would. Her only daughter. But Mary died, and the new baby died too, about a week after Mary.

Slowly the memory of the pain spread its lament across her, louder and more overwhelming than what she could bear without screaming out, like the crier's voice now returned in her direction: "It's starting now! The parade is starting at once!"

Ben came to the funeral too. In her mind she sees the coffin Norman made of split pine logs; a white sheet wrapping her daughter's body, John singing a Cree hymn — melancholy as a loon behind the horizon's last light — the pasty yellow soil lining a hole John's brothers dug at a clearing's edge. These images were burned into her memory.

Ben held her hand that day to help her climb into their democrat. He put his arm around her shoulder for a while as they headed back to Morley, young Sitting Wind, now coming to live with them, asleep on canvas and gear behind the seat. Ben listened in silence to her account of how Wind had once healed the boy. "He will be a great leader," she emphasized, as if trying to persuade him.

It has been sixteen years now since Moraha moved in with Ben Kaquitts at Morley. It was soon after Ben's former wife died, when he traveled to Hobbema to ask her.

Ben had a log cabin with a flat wood floor at Chiniki Village on the Stoney reserve. "The Indian Agent who worked with us Stoneys arranged to bring in milled boards on the fire-wagon, straight to the Morley Station," Ben chuckled. The other Stoneys living there were friendly.

"Horses are saddled and ready. It's time to go now."

The door flap is thrown open, silhouetting Ben in a blinding shaft of morning sun. She draws a colourfully printed kerchief over her head, knotting it under her chin. She is ready.

Four-year-old Sitting Wind has sensed her mood and has remained seated quietly on his bedding, waiting for her. Mechanically she takes him by the hand, nudging him ahead, outside. He is wearing dusty and crumpled dungarees, and a checkered shirt and moccasins like those of his step-grandfather, Ben. His hair has grown considerably, and she made small braids for him too — reaching below the shoulder — tying their ends off with short thongs. It shows he's an Indian, she smiles wanly to herself.

It is a clear morning near the end of July. Is she a little slower than usual today? The sun is already high, its direct rays warm on the doors of fifty colourful tepees erected in a long arc along the ground's west perimeter. The large meadow is alive with activity: Stoney women and men, many wearing beads and some with head-dresses, children, mongrel dogs and small waddling pups, horses with ponies in tow, and a scattering of wagons.

And there are the onlookers. People from all over Canada and the United States, enticed by brightly painted Canadian Pacific Railway posters in their home towns which beckon them to come and soak in hot springs, to ride in mountains, and to see Indians. True Indians living like they did in old days before settlers came. As Moraha and little Sitting Wind emerge from their tepee into heat and dust, several tourists draw up.

To maintain some privacy, however tenuous, Moraha pretends not to take notice. Ben has brought their horses nearby, dropping their reins to the dirt to discourage the animals from wandering. Buzzing flies hover about their glossy eyes. Ben was unhappy about not being permitted to keep their wagon in close to the tepee, but Norman Luxton, the organizer, has forbidden it because white people like to photograph tepees with Minay Rhappa in the background.

"Hello, my dear. Isn't it just a grand day?" The voice belongs to a woman with shiny white-strapped shoes on her feet, a cotton print dress, and a floppy-brimmed hat falling over her ears.

"And what a beautiful wigwam you have." Her sparkling blue eyes are directed past Moraha at the two half-moons of hunting season which Ben painted over the door two years ago. Many tourists say "wigwams". On one occasion someone asked to look inside her wigwam and she was afraid to say yes because she didn't know what was meant. She smiles pleasantly at the woman's comment, but keeps her eyes half to the ground. Not that she minds their interest; they are always nice. But she doesn't feel comfortable making unnecessary conversation.

"You wouldn't mind if we take a snap of your little girl, would you? She looks just darling. Doesn't she, Christopher?" A man sporting short, slicked back hair nods enthusiastically while fumbling with a black box in his hand.

Moraha attempts a more avid smile and looks down at Sitting Wind. He does have charm about him. Most tourists believe only girls have braids, but she is becoming accustomed to this mistake.

"He is a boy," she says apologetically.

"Oh, I'm sorry!" The woman bends with laughter. "How could I possibly make such an error?"

Sitting Wind clearly loves to have attention showered on him. At moments like this Moraha has no regrets about having needed to take the grandchild into her household.

Sometimes the tourists seem ignorant about us Indians. They may even think he is my own child, she muses.

The powerful Stoney seer, Hector Crawler, once warned them about photos. They are strong medicine, he said, and could be used to hurt you with magic.

"It's all right." The woman has detected her hesitation. "You see, it's for the Queen. She loves to see her Indian friends far away, and she will be very happy to see you in a photograph since she cannot come here herself."

Moraha, unaware that the woman has been told that this is an effective tactic, envisions the crowned Queen sitting in a high-backed throne, flanked by draping Union Jacks and staring at the photo approvingly. Ben is already at Moraha's horse and appears to be waiting.

"Here, you little cutie. Simply stand for a moment between these other two children, and Christopher will snap your photograph." The woman is tugging Sitting Wind's arm and standing him between Dillon Rider and one of the Hunter children. Moraha cannot resist now. It would cause a scene.

"I want you all to remain very still. Give me a big smile now!" chatters the slick man. His smooth chin creases against his brown bow tie as his eyes train through the box-top. After a suspense-filled pause it eventually clicks, and he stands erect again, children dispersing to the cover of mothers' skirts. They glance back in a jingle of giggles to see what may transpire next.

Moraha leads Sitting Wind to her horse and travois. Ben is waiting to help. She deftly pulls herself up onto a blanket strapped into the curve of the Cayuse's back, while her husband lifts the two children, Sitting Wind and his friend Dillon, into their cleverly designed travois nest.

"The capes! Where are their eagle-baby capes?" The face of Dillon's mother appears, with a mixture of concern and mischief. Moraha's hand comes to her mouth in embarrassment. She has forgotten to bring out the down-covered capes Rachel made for Dillon and Sitting Wind.

"In the tepees!" she calls.

Quickly the young woman gathers them from a peg inside and slips them over the youngsters' heads, nods and hoots of approval echoing from a small crowd now gathering around. The youngsters are transformed into downy eagle fledglings huddled in a fur-lined nest.

"Give them these bags too." Moraha's voice is directed at her husband, Ben, as she hands him two cloth sugar bags. He must think she is rather disorganized this morning. More people gather around, admiring the innovative travois. In their native tongue, Ben instructs the youngsters how to hold open their bags to receive donations.

In a way Stoneys are fortunate, compared to Moraha's Cree relatives back home on the reserve of her birth. Stoneys have a good thing here — free buffalo meat, flour, tea, whiteman's jam, bread, sugar, and snacks of all sorts donated by the Canadian Pacific Railway, hotels, and other Banff businesses.

On the one hand, whitemen are friendly like us Indians, she tells herself. They share things like we Indians do. On the other hand they seem to be continually occupying more land. The Indians are only on small reserves. Every year around Morley new fences are going up. When we question, we always get the same reply — "This is not Indian land" — regardless of the fact that Stoneys have been hunting there and grazing horses there as long as can be remembered. When will it end? Where will it lead?

Why do they offer us these other gifts year after year? Is it because they desire to be friends? They are friendly, but it confuses her. They are clever, and they can argue persuasively. They know things. And every year there seem to be still more people watching, poking, questioning. It dismays her. Where do they all come from? The lands far away must be very large to contain so many people.

Moraha blocks out the turmoil around her, her thoughts drifting back to Hobbema. John will be having a hard time now, alone, looking after Sitting Wind's older brothers, those five ruffian boys. There's no way he will be able to manage. He will need to take another wife immediately. Moraha herself has done her part, what seemed only sensible, by taking four-year-old Sitting Wind with her to Morley. He is too young to stay in a family without a mother.

Someone relays a signal. Her calves squeeze against the cayuse's sides and it hinges forward into a familiar swaying gait. The movement is soothing. She could as well be out in wilderness hunting, or on her way to a new camp somewhere. Automatically she follows Ben's horse, poles furrowing unevenly through dry sod behind her. The laughter of the kids mingling with summer dust tells her there's no urgent need to look back toward the countless high pitched voices, showering compliments. Other horses also are moving, converging to the race track near the gate, some harnessed into democrats containing whole families. She picks out her brother-in-law, Pete Poucette, riding an Appaloosa and leading a packhorse loaded with a bundle of blankets and furs. A younger lad she doesn't recognize is sporting a tassled smoked buckskin jacket and a tall stetson. Another's costume is a comical composite of dance and show attire. It seems out of place, she muses, with a porcupine roach swaying above a bleached and brightly beaded jacket.

Although he has not said so, she has sensed that Ben did not want to have little Sitting Wind move in with them. But what else was to be done? Of course she can understand his attitude, since Sitting Wind is her family, her grandchild, and not related to Ben at all. She respects Ben for remaining silent on this subject, and hopes that he will eventually accept what must be.

Ben has circled around into his appropriate place near the front of the line-up behind chiefs and councilmen. Two RCMP at the very lead stand erect as statues, their scarlet tunics slotted into polished saddle brims, silver spurs on black boots tight to the flanks of their dark mink horses.

The animals immediately following them are decorated with beadwork and carry the three Stoney chiefs trailing long bonnets of eagle feathers: Hector Crawler of the Chiniki Band, Jonas Rider of the Bearspaw Band, and Jonas Benjamin of the Goodstoney Band. The councilmen are behind the chiefs, followed by more wildly costumed young men. The women and children take up the rear. The Bearspaw chief knows how to sit tall; he was a champion cowboy at the Calgary Stampede in earlier years.

As the sun's heat begins to penetrate her clothes, Moraha suppresses a strained yawn. Sleep came late last night. In the evening Joshua Wildman started off the pow-wow with a drum-dance song. This was followed by an owl dance, and later there were war dances, and chicken dances involving larger groups of Indians circling round and round in a kaleidoscope of smiles, dust, and colour.

"Come and dance with me, and we'll make ourselves happy," Ben's sister prodded her, teasing. "It is not good to grieve for ones you miss after they are buried." She was right. And it was fun too. Paul Amos led a deer dance. The Creator provides wild game such as deer for survival — for meat and clothing, for everything required. By doing this dance they ask the Creator to bring deer.

The parade proceeds slowly along Banff Avenue, as it does every year, toward the Banff Springs Hotel. Toward town, on the Bow River bridge, the Mounties stop and wait. The entire parade comes to a halt, people crowding close around the travois, as Moraha, in her section, waits before the Mount Royal Hotel. The children are happy, a continuous jangle of coins dropping into their bags.

She supposes that, at one time, judging of costumes and parade entries did not occur. Moraha has identified the three judges, her eyes looking sideways. Their shoes are glossed, and they walk like bosses, nodding to familiar Stoney friends. One has a moustache like squirrel tails over his lip. Another is a friendly woman, named Pearl Moore. The three scrutinize each horse, each person. The three pairs of eyes each in turn survey Moraha's horse and clothing from bottom to top. They will say some Stoneys are better than others and they will give them special honour. Moraha is reminded how inadequate her attire is this year.

Although young Dillon is relaxed with the crowds, Sitting Wind's young eyes are wide with the novelty of such unrelenting activity around him — not only all these people, but also the town itself. Never before has he seen so many buildings side by side. One of them, the Alberta Hotel, is taller than trees and has three or four windows in a row, one above another.

"Here you are, fifty cents: a quarter for each of you! Most adorable little fellows!" The bag is becoming heavy, and Dillon can manage only to point its mouth in the direction of a yellow patterned dress flaring out over high heels. Others push in closer around the boys. He smells the perfume of young flowers.

"Look at these two little birds! The epitome of Nature's perfect innocence! Don't you agree, Norm? You really must take a snapshot of them. Look at those natural tans underneath their feathers, and those mysterious dark eyes." Perhaps she wants to kiss him with her glossy lips on his face, or kidnap him. The curls alongside her earrings appear inviting to touch.

Excited voices shout from up above him and Sitting Wind's eyes search for their origin among flags, mostly red, thrust out from walls and flapping lazily like great geese. The windows of the Mount Royal Hotel contain glass, reflecting blue sky and an occasional wisp of white cloud. There they are: people's heads and arms strain over ledges, pointing. He wonders how they climb so high up.

"The whitemen are way up there, Grandma?" He screeches the half question, pointing.

Moraha turns in her blanket-saddle. The child's voice drags her back from Hobbema and her despondency. She has seen taller buildings in Calgary, near the Stampede grounds where they go, each year, to camp in the Indian Village. They could not attend the Stampede this year — because of Mary. Moraha could have used the money, four dollars a day for each tepee, but Mary was more important.

"They make these big houses with stones, one on top of another." She tries to explain. "Tall like mountains. They make rooms one on top of the other, with tunnels to climb between them."

Sitting Wind marvels at this. He imagines white women with their long dresses and bunchberry hats scrambling up steep dark tunnels on hands and knees.

The judges return. Their eyes have stopped roving; they are resolute, in control.

"What's your name?" The one with the long waxed moustache stops beside Moraha's dangling leg. He is writing on paper.

"Mrs Ben Kaquitts."

"You have won a prize for the best travois. A wonderful job, I should add. Congratulations."

He ties a brilliant red ribbon to the halter and hands her twenty dollars, the crowd cheering behind him. She wishes she had made beads on the halter, and the rope is too dirty and plain. But Ben will be happy, proud. Coins continue falling behind her into the sugar-bags and into the nest, some jangling to pavement, rolling. Cameras are clicking, attacking. Waves of smiles, smiles with bristle hairs, with lipstick, with blue pimples, with hats, with rouge, advancing and retreating, circling like water beneath falls that continue day and night. The children are churring with glee.

The horse jerks into motion again. The museum falls away to her right, filled with animal spirits caged behind glass. They cross a bridge over the river, cold water flowing luxuriously beneath. She imagines the parade fording the water, as it may have done in past years. Horses would enjoy cool water penetrating crevices of their hoofs, and would drink with long satisfying sucks.

Shortly, around a bend in the road, the most colossal house Sitting Wind has ever seen slides into view: the Banff Springs Hotel. It towers above him as they draw closer, like a mountain, but with rows upon rows of windows. Tilting his head back, he looks straight up to where a roof-line separates the structure from passing clouds, and he experiences an alarming sense of loss of balance. His hands clench the travois bars and he jerks his eyes away, toward Grandma's back. Could this building be tipping? But Grandma doesn't seem alarmed.

Sitting Wind allows his eyes to climb again. There are whitemen with their hands over ledges watching the parade. They are not afraid either.

Around back of the hotel, the entourage funnels through a gate into a fenced courtyard, horses mingling in confusion. Thousands of faces attach themselves to fences, eagerly probing small wire squares with fingers, noses and eyes. The chiefs dismount in the center and sit in a circle on a platform with some whitemen. Norman Luxton raises his hand.

"Ladies and gentlemen, if you please. Your attention! Your attention please!" The babbling subsides, broken only by bawling of babies and the occasional flubbering of a horse.

"It is my privilege again on this last day of the fortieth anniversary of Banff Indian Days to say a few words."

Moraha has dismounted and is seated on a bench near the cool wall of limestone blocks. Her Cayuse is content to stand still now, one hind leg pulled up slightly, head hanging. The youngsters are absorbed with pulling feathers from each other's faces and swinging them in small arcs over their heads. The loudspeakers, mounted on corners of the platform, bounce the crackling words from building walls into mountainsides and trees, and spill them into the Bow River gorge.

"First of all I wish to introduce to you the greatest chiefs of the Stoney Indian Tribe standing beside me here: Chief Hector Crawler, Chief Jonas Rider, and Chief Jonas Benjamin. I thank them, as I'm sure you all do, for bringing their people to Banff this year in such large numbers. I think we should all show them our sincere appreciation." The crowd breaks into a wave of applause, like wind in dry tops of autumn poplars.

"On this day they have asked me to explain the importance of the Peace Treaty to our Indian people. When in 1877, Her Majesty the Queen of England made a sacred treaty with the Indians of our magnificent land, she did so because she desired a true and lasting peace. Peace among Indians and peace between Indians and whites. Well, I have had occasion to live with these people here: my Indian friends. They are my brothers. And I can assure you all, without a shadow of doubt, that they are the most law abiding and peace loving people on the face of the earth. For this reason I wish you to consider them your friends as well. Banff Indian Days are an opportunity for you to show your friendship. To show them welcome. Thank you."

The crowd breaks into applause once more. Again Mr Luxton raises his hand for silence.

"One announcement please before the parade is dispersed. A reminder that races at the Indian Days Grounds commence at two o'clock sharp. The price is only one dollar for adults, twenty five cents for children, all moneys going to the Indians. First on the agenda will be Indian pony races. If you have not seen these before, I can assure you that they are unforgettable: sinuous braves galloping their wild steeds with a most reckless abandon right to the finish line. Following this will be foot races, archery, and the other thrilling events in which these people excel."

The podium empties quickly after hand shakes, and the crowd around collapses into animated turmoil. Some waiters and waitresses weave through the Indians with trays of chocolates, fruit, cigarettes, and cookies. Sitting Wind's and Dillon's mouths stain brown, and chocolate invades the fringes of goose-down sown to their capes.

"Did we get money from the whiteman, Grandma?" Sitting Wind asks later, back at the tepee, as Moraha peels the feathered costume from him.

"Yes, they liked how you and Dillon looked in your travois. That's why they gave us money."

"Can we get some candy and ice cream with money?"

"Yes. Here is some for each of you. But come right back." She offers them coins from the sugar-bag, for ice cream. Sitting Wind is happy.

"Does it mean whitemen are nice for giving us money?"

"Yes. They give us things."

Moraha lies down on her bedding, although the air inside is stifling, heavy under burning sun. Ben is busy with the horses.

"I like whiteman's ice cream," Sitting Wind says as he exits. "I'm gonna buy some chocolate, too.''

Moraha squeezes her eyelids shut, tears spilling along wrinkles which radiate from their corners. She will be a good mother for this child. Mary would want her to be a good mother for Sitting Wind. If only Mary could see her boy now and then, and be happy for him.

Indian Flats, Canmore
August, 1929

Young Sitting Wind awakens with a start. The dog outside the tepee is barking hoarsely and relentlessly. The summer night within the mountains is crisp, black.

"What is it out there? Huh? Quit making noise, crazy pup. You'll make the horses nervous."

Sitting Wind recognizes Grandpa Ben's low, reassuring voice behind the canvas. He hears the dog too, scurrying this way and that, feet padding turf, breathing, snuffling. Grandpa must be teasing it or playing with it: the sounds come in short, intense volleys interspersed with curious interludes of silence.

Lying on his back and now fully alert, the child's open eyes adjust to the dimly lit interior. A column of blue smoke rising from the fire circle slowly funnels toward the vent, accelerating and thinning, being sucked up and through into night air. Ends of stark lodge-poles criss-cross over bright stars shimmering in a black beyond.

A momentary lull is interrupted as Ben growls and spituees, ejecting a stream of tobacco juice. The dog sniffs noisily. Sitting Wind hears the sound of urine dribbling to the soil. Silence again.

Finally, there's a ruffling of the door-flap as Grandpa re-enters. Sitting Wind lowers his eyes over an unwashed nose, raising his head slightly; the shadows cast by Grandpa's body settling back into place by the fire are like ghosts sweeping the canvas. He hears him grunt. The sounds are like words, but they are short, incomplete, and his grandma, Moraha, whose face he can now make out in the glow of a small flame, remains immobile. If Grandpa communicated something, she shows no response. Sitting Wind traces the deep lines of her face, warm with the orange reflection. She seems happy. Composed.

It was a vague ennui that invaded his sleep. Images of his mother Mary repeatedly formed in his mind. He saw her sitting like Grandma, by the fire. Saw her stitching tiny blue beads onto a pair of moccasins, his pair, special for show and for dancing, stitching a big bird with out-stretched wings onto each foot. But her face was chalk: white like fresh buckskin, and flat. He had never seen her face flat like that. A white sheet persistently circled around her, trapping her; she struggled weakly against it. He wanted to help, but his small arms were powerless, could not reach. Father's voice commanded ''Quiet''. His brother Paul repeated ''Quiet''. And even Ed right after him echoed ''Quiet'', in a smaller voice, attempting authority that did not become him. Women were wailing. They were in a different house at Hobbema: not his home cabin where they lived, but in another field.

Now awake, and finding Grandpa and Grandma relaxed, he feels reassured. Early this morning they dismantled the Indian Days camp, loaded tepee cover, stove, and supplies on the democrat and headed down the Bow Valley with Grandma's horse in tow. These trips are fun, riding high in the democrat, perched on the seat or on top of the gear — the endless shapes and contours of the majestic mountains looming up on both sides. There are such varied textures of forest: smears of grey scree descending from the upper ends of avalanche slopes and grading to soft green at their toes; broad patches of dark-needled trees interspersed with lighter leafy stands in valley bottoms; dry, bouldery creek beds passing under the road; and glimpses of the wide Bow River (Mnee Thnay, or Cold Water, in Stoney) travelling like a friend alongside them, pointing the way to Morley.

Grandma kept him good company, enjoying a new youthful presence in her life.

''Wesakijak made those,'' she piped up. She pointed with her mouth, pursing her lips like Stoneys do into a wrinkled otter nose and directing them, as if she were throwing a kiss, at hoodoos rising tall against an eroded valley wall. He visualized the legendary giant standing there, so much taller than the trees that they were like grass at his feet.

''Who is Wesakijak?'' he asked. Not that he didn't already know. He simply wanted to hear it again. Each time he hears it he can better anticipate the string of events, one after another. And, while wagon wheels continued jolting and crushing over the gravel trail, Grandma patiently recounted the tale of how Wesakijak, the giant, fun-loving superman of long ago, created mountains and rivers and all things. And how at last he also made a person, an Indian.

''After he made people he let us live our own lives of hunting deer and digging roots. But one day, during the coldest of all winters, he was playing around in this area and he noticed we had no house to live in, to hide away in from cold and snow. So he scooped some nearby dirt into a pile making a tall hoodoo, the largest one you can see, right over there.''

She directed his gaze at the largest cone. He could see where gravel had been scooped from a creek bed, cupped in Wesakijac's great hands.

"Wesakijac felt sorry for us. That's why he did this. He told people that from now on these are your tepees. He told them to go inside and be safe from the cold. Later, people began making tepees out of poles and animal hides."

Sitting Wind searched for an entrance, but it was hidden from view.

His eyes study a dancing of firelight along canvas above his nose, shadowy tongues darting like chicken dancers at a pow-wow, twisting, gyrating, round and around. The canvas darkens with soot toward the vent. Some stray smoke causes him to sneeze.

"Has he woken up?" Grandpa's voice mutters from the shadows. A blanket ruffles softly and Grandma's arm comes around, her blotched brown eyes suddenly searching directly into Sitting Wind's. Her breath is a steam of sweet dry-meat, acid buffalo berries, and rich tobacco.

"I'm awake now," he says faintly. "But it is still night, isn't it?"

"Come to the fire, my son. Maybe you're not tired enough." Grandpa says it as if he is tracking a moose, and is coming within earshot. "I will tell some stories for you to remember as you grow older."

Sitting Wind wraps his blanket about the shoulders and tilts himself over against Grandma's hip. He waits, studying Grandpa's scarred and weathered face. Grandpa's eyes are lost in the fire, searching corners of his best memories.

Moraha lowers a heavy arm around the child. She has heard Ben's stories before, but she enjoys hearing them again, reviewing them and retasting morsels of suspense, of humour, of surprise. He addressed the boy as "son". She smokes her pipe, the one from Nordegg. Ben begins to speak.

"A short distance from this camp here, on the bank of Mnee Thnay river is a place with whitemen's houses. They dig coal from the ground there too, for the fire-wagon riding on steel tracks. The whitemen name this place Canmore." Grandpa spits into the fire. "But we Stoneys name it Chuamp Chip Chiyehn Kuday Be."

"A long time ago there was a war party of twelve Stoneys roaming around through the mountains some distance from here, to the west. They were looking to fight enemies, paint on their faces." Grandpa is expressive when he tells stories; when he says "roaming around" he snakes his arm through the air horizontally, and when he says "paint on their faces'' he rakes his cheek with thick leathery fingers.

''They were lucky and found some Blackfoot and fought them at the bottom of the Cascade Valley near Minay Wanka.'' (Minay means ''lake''; wanka means ''spirit'': Lake Minnewanka.)

''In those days we Stoneys were known by other tribes as 'head cutters' because we were more fierce and stronger than any of them. These bloodthirsty braves caught one of the enemy, bang! bang! and cut off his head. But the other Blackfoot all escaped. The Stoneys were hungry for blood; they were not satisfied with just one. They wanted to chase them and kill them all, cutting off their heads: cut! cut! cut!'' Grandpa chops his hand through the air like an axe. ''So they divided themselves into two groups to search for those who slipped away. One group rode toward where the sun sets, up a valley to Cuthead Creek, but the others went toward where the sun rises, this way down Mnee Thnay valley.

''This second group travelled all afternoon, this way and that, looking for the tracks of enemy horses or any other sign to betray their whereabouts. Finally they became so exhausted that it was necessary to stop and sleep: sleep forced itself upon them, even though the remaining enemies had not been found, and could be lurking somewhere nearby.

''They made a hasty camp in a clearing near the river, and decided to take turns sleeping while some kept watch. Their camp was very close to where we are tonight.

''First they tied their horses immediately beside the tepee to prevent their theft. Then, those who were chosen to sleep first slid into the tepee and nodded off instantly. The others kept watch, although they were so tired that their eyes were strained. But they forced themselves to stay awake, taking no chance on being ambushed by surprise.

''In the middle of night one of the watchmen thought he heard a noise near camp: some crackling of bushes. He listened more carefully for a time, keeping himself in the shadows. But the noise passed. Everything was quiet. Still, it made him nervous. He began to reflect on it. He became suspicious that possibly the remaining Blackfoot warriors had discovered their camp, and were now preparing to avenge the death of their headless brother. They were probably hiding in the shadows of trees, plotting, making silent signals to one another with sinuous hands. He peered into the darkness, staring at any shadow to see if it would move now and then. Even the air shifting among leaves began to sound like enemies creeping about, whispering too loud, making ready to charge, hideous death songs shrieking as they converged on him. He began to sense he was a sitting target.

"If these are our enemies all around us we are surely doomed, he thought. Even the silence began to take on meaning. He began to consider: maybe they are playing a game first before they kill us, to see if we will be afraid. His instinct was to wake up the others and warn them, but that would show fear. What if their tracks are not found? His brothers would make fun of him, saying he is a coward, scared. No he would not wake them. He would face them bravely, even at night. So he continued listening and staring into the darkness surrounding the circle of their camp.

"Suddenly his eyes made out a more distinct shadow. It appeared to be a Blackfoot, crouching perhaps. He stared long and hard, his pupils so wide that they burned, and yes, it began to move a little, wavering. That must be one of them murderous dogs, he thought. When he could contain himself no longer he called out to it.

"'Who is there?'" Grandpa's dramatically loud bellow startles Sitting Wind.

"There was no answer. Of course there was no answer. It would be foolish to answer if he was an enemy. Now the Stoney brave was convinced it was one of them. It had to be.

"He raised his thirty-thirty expertly, smoothly, and squeezed the trigger. Boom!" Grandpa's hand comes down into his palm. "He shot again. Boom! Boom! And the figure's stature was halved, if not more. He's dead now; he must be dead now. If not, he is mortally wounded and will surely be dead in a moment, the brave thought. But he did not dare to go and see in case the other Blackfoot were still around. Let the others also come to me, he thought. I will wait for them and finish them all.

"'What are you shooting at?' cried his brothers from the tepee.

"'I shot one of the enemy in the trees,' he replied proudly, holding his breath to disguise his pounding heart. 'I don't think they will bother us now!'

"In the morning, when the sky began to light up, they approached the site to find the body and cut off the head. Although they searched carefully everywhere, they could find no tracks. Finally, they discovered shreds of bark where bullets had smashed a small tree.

"Immediately they realized what had taken place. They laughed at their brother, saying he must be afraid of death to be shooting at anything that moves, to be shooting a small tree in the dark because he thought it was one of the enemy.

"That is why we call this place Chuamp Chip Chiyehn Kuday Be," Grandpa finishes. "It means, 'The place where he shot a small tree.'"

Grandpa laughs from his chest, and Grandma laughs too, with her hand to her mouth, although the firelight is weak and there is no one else there to see her. Sitting Wind's mind, now more fully alert, and at the same time still bewildered by his family's fragmentation, begins imagining the enemy's head lying cold on the ground in darkness, like a sinister boulder with shiny whites of eyes staring up at an autumn moon.

But, almost as quickly, these gloomy images are interrupted by the dog outside, whining almost inaudibly. The long silence following the story is part of it, part of its enjoyment, required for its digestion. Grandma and Grandpa seem to be lapsing into a trance, into another world. Sitting Wind's ears listen for the pup's breath of resignation, but he cannot hear it. The pup is lonely, he thinks. It whines again, softly. There is no wind. There are other tepees in the meadow, but they are soundless. It must be very late.

A coyote's wail splits the silence, first rising to a high pitch and then falling into a slow, mournful howl.

"Coyote," he verbalizes. Hearing his own voice seems to confirm its identity, and this immediately stifles his alarm. The elders continue to sit mute, mesmerized. The silence following its howl is even more total in contrast, and Sitting Wind listens intently for a slight sound to betray the animal's whereabouts; the accidental snapping of a small twig, or rustling of a dry leaf.

The howl cuts again, like lightning, and others farther away join in a luxuriant chorus that begins to linger. It hangs like crystal rain in the trees, in the cliffs, in the sky all around, bouncing like light beams on shimmering wavelets everywhere: a symphony of yapping and screaming, filling the air, the tepee, filling his entire being as if he were hollow.

Then the coyotes' sounds fade away as quickly as they appeared. Grandma stirs and puffs her pipe, spits sour tar into the fire. Grandpa watches it sizzle and shrink to nothing on an ember. He wipes his mouth with a sleeve.

"The following day the braves caught up with the remaining enemies, and killed them all cruelly," Grandpa finishes at last.

"Now, I will tell you a different story. One which took place not many years ago, right in this very camp where we are sleeping tonight. This camping site is called Tinda Meemum which means Round Clearing. The whitemen call it Indian Flats because they often see us camping here.

"There are many deer in this area, and grouse, rabbits, and beavers. Also, less snow falls here than elsewhere. A great Stoney Medicine Man whose name was Suzay, and who lived many many years ago, told us to preserve the game in this area for special occasions, for emergency weather conditions. It's all right to camp here anytime, he said, but do not kill any game in the vicinity of these flats. He told us the Bow Valley between Morley and Banff was not to be hunted except in desperation, when we are starving.

"But this is not yet my story." Grandpa chuckles at the way he has gently misdirected their suspense. His chuckle is throaty, rasping, from inhaling greasy tepee smoke for more than sixty years.

"The story is about another time, when some Stoneys were camped here. It takes place during the Tah Keeyorha Waheeyumba (Moose Mating Season). There were about five tepees camped together here on route to a hunting trip in the Yarhey Tinda (Mountain Plain) area. Everyone was happy, eager for hunting to begin, preparing dry-meat, and bringing back hides for new clothes and handicrafts.

"Among one of the families there was a young girl who was approaching puberty. She was very beautiful. Her father guarded her closely because many young men had their eyes on her. One day she slipped away. She told her mother, 'I'm going to gather some bearberries for when we make pemmican.' Her mother was happy that her daughter had this idea. She had noticed fat berries this year, vigorously red.

"The girl was absent most of the afternoon and then her father became worried. 'Where can she be?' he complained. 'She should be tired of picking berries by now.' He went to investigate, calling in various directions as he searched through pale aspens and gravelly clearings. But he was unable to locate her. When he returned, unsuccessful, both parents went out to look, but still they were unable to find her. Other relatives, and soon all available people in camp, began searching for her. When eventually the sky grew dark, she was still not found, and her mother began to cry; her sisters and cousins also began to cry, believing she was killed by an animal. For two days they searched all over the mountainside above the Flats, but the girl who went berry-picking was nowhere to be found.

"Finally they hired a medicine man to divine from Spirits what may have befallen her. He rode from Morley, carrying a small drum. Immediately when he received a message that there was an emergency at Tinda Meemum, he stopped eating so that his communication with Spirits would be successful. Upon arrival he constructed a sweat lodge in the clump of aspen nearby, using red willows near the river. He prepared hot rocks in a small fire close to the door, and carried them inside to make steam. He drummed and chanted, hour after hour. He prayed to his Spirit, 'Spirit, enter my body, give your servant a dream, a vision, so these parents may learn what has happened to their beloved daughter.'

"Meanwhile, the parents were waiting impatiently for him to emerge. They had waited almost half a day when finally the tiny door opened and the medicine man re-appeared, sweat dripping from his naked torso, eyes gaunt. He raised a hand for attention.

"'The Spirits have now answered my prayers and given me the message we have anxiously been awaiting,' he said. 'They have told me there is no need to worry any more, nor do you need to search for your daughter anymore, because she has been found and is in good hands. This is what the Spirits have said today.

"'Your daughter has been captured by some little-people who dwell in cliffs nearby this camp. The Spirits have confirmed that these little-people have been waiting for a princess for many years, not to kill her or do her any harm, but that she may rule over them. Now she is their queen and will not become old for a long time. Nor will she become sick. She will be happy. The only difficulty is that she will never see her parents anymore. Rest assured however, she agreed to go along with the little-people once they explained this to her. She realizes she will be very happy with them, receiving from them everything she desires.'

"The medicine man then led the people up on the bench above camp where he pointed to tracks in clay washed into crevices between seams of gravel: the tracks of these little-people being merely three or four inches long. He pointed to the larger tracks of the girl between those of little people: they were double the others' size.

"'What we see here,' he explained, 'are tracks of at least two, maybe three little-people. They walked alongside her, leading her away.'

"The young men attempted to follow the tracks, but when they reached ledges of exposed bedrock the faint impressions disappeared.

"Little-people live inside the mountain in caves," Grandpa said to Sitting Wind in an aside. "You will be made aware of them if you approach too close to their homes, by small rocks falling or wind suddenly starting up." Then he continued with the story.

"Once the medicine man explained the truth, everyone stopped searching for her. Thereafter, the parents worried less; of course, they were lonely for her, but they consoled themselves by remembering that she was happy, and that nothing could be done to bring her back. After that day, girls and boys were not permitted to wander by themselves in this area; they were warned to go in pairs, or groups."

Grandpa's silence marks the end of this story. But Sitting Wind's appetite is young, eager for more.

"Tell me another story, Grandpa," he begs with large eyes. He wonders if little-people ever descend from the rocks into the camping meadow.

"That's all the stories for tonight," Grandpa pronounces with finality. Grandma's chin has fallen forward onto her chest.

"I'll mention now the places through which we will pass tomorrow on our way to Morley, and then you will sleep."

"First, a short distance east from this meadow, we pass Chassay Eempah (Dry Timber Ridge) where wind and sun make dry firewood any time of year. One can find sheep there when the weather is cold. This is the first place we will pass, right above Gap Lake.

"A little farther east from Chassay Eempah, a creek emerges from the mountains at a place whitemen call Exshaw, shortly before we pass through the Park Gate. We call this place Chappay Oday, the Place of Many Stumps."

Sitting Wind recalls passing through the Park Gate on their way to Banff Indian Days the week before, large clean-shaven logs fastened together in a magnificent arch over the road.

"When I was younger, this place was a thick woods, full of pine and spruce fed by the creek. But the Lime Pit, located near the Park Gate, used to pay us money for firewood and this is how we came to cut trees there every year. Eventually all trees were cut, leaving an open field of stumps.

"After passing through the Park Gate, we will be close to our reserve."

James River
September, 1929

Sitting Wind lifts a drooping branch, carefully avoiding the nasty thorns the way Moraha, his grandma, demonstrated the day before, and exposes an array of sweet gooseberries suspended beneath. He is almost five years old now, an astute learner. He wants to try things by himself.

Yesterday afternoon they went out and picked saskatoons; his fingers were sticky purple. Without prickles, the saskatoon bushes are friendlier than these.

"It's a good year for berries," Grandma laughed. They carried their harvest back to camp, a pail full — Sitting Wind found a rusty pail in trees behind the tepee — and Grandma spread them on a canvas to dry in the sun.

"When they are dry," she explained, "they cannot spoil, and they will be lighter to carry around."

Now, among the gooseberries, his wool leggings persistently catch on nasty horizontal branches below eye level. The juices are tangy behind his gums, on the inside walls of his cheeks. But it does not deter him; on the contrary, he craves more, gingerly lifting another promising branch.

"Sitting Wind! Come on now! Sitting Wind! What are you doing!" Grandma sounds impatient. She is a short distance ahead of him, standing squat in the center of the trail. Dangling poplar leaves fluttering in his line of sight fracture her image. The brilliant noon sky makes the leaves appear polished like thousands of little green beads bobbling. She does not see him yet. Hastily, he gathers a few more fat berries and pops them into his mouth, the slippery contents squishing between his teeth as he bites down, sucking.

The leggings are made from sleeves of an old wool coat, chafing ties wrapped around his waist. Underneath are his shorts and a breach cloth which was once a small blanket or towel. Grandma spied the material on a shelf at the Morley Trading Post, and her arthritic fingers fumbled for the dollar tucked into her dress. The deerskin vest, hanging loosely over his small torso, was lovingly constructed long ago by his mother Mary. It is now greasy brown, impregnated with heavy tanning smoke and sweat. It is his favourite — he saw other kids wear similar ones at Indian Days. The old moccasins on his feet are too large, so Grandma helped tie their thongs extra snug.

It is fun going for lunch with Grandpa and the men; Grandma has said that soon he will be old enough to help repair fences.

Grandma is backtracking, looking for him. She has had enough. The crook of her right arm is bent around a bag containing dry-meat, flour, and tea. Her other hand clutches the neck of a blanket bag slung over her shoulder and containing a frying pan, tea pot, and other supplies. The men will be hungry, having been out since first light this morning.

She knows they would prefer berry pemmican because it yields more energy, with its rich fat melted into dried meat fibers. But the berries need two or three hot days for drying. They will appreciate it all the more, she tells herself, having to wait a few extra days. It's a good thing the rancher has work for them; they need the money.

"Here I am, Grandma! I'm coming!" Sitting Wind bounces onto the trail. She is so close, she would have discovered him any second.

"Where did you leave the water crock? Pay attention! You should not forget the water crock someplace, or we shall all be thirsty!" Ben would be very upset if the youngster were to spill their water along the way, or to lose the jug somewhere. The timing would not be good; not at this point.

Although she is older now, Moraha enjoys these autumn wilderness excursions away from the reserve more than ever before in her life. She loves the challenge of living in harmony, nothing more complex than a slow inhaling and exhaling of earth and elements. She is especially pleased with this opportunity to teach young Sitting Wind old ways of survival, to prepare him for his life and the future.

In recent decades, some Stoneys have grown accustomed to remaining on the reserve year-round. They have become afraid of the government; its agents, rangers, officers are always stopping and asking for a permit, a license, some proof that you are doing nothing wrong, and that you are not in an illegal place. She recalls that they once had to possess a permit simply for being off the reserve. They make you feel guilty, as if you have committed wrong, killed somebody, or stolen something.

She remembers one time watching Ben's son, Josiah, shoot a deer. Although he was in a proper hunting area she noticed how nervous he suddenly became, casting about this way and that before pulling the trigger, and butchering rapidly, furtively. This is not right, she later thought. It is not right that the young men are afraid to kill their food. How else will they survive?

But there are some, like Ben himself, who remain restless travellers, eager to head out each fall for work with local ranchers. If they are needed, that is. And afterward they go hunting and trapping. As soon as the permit system was abandoned, Ben began hunting again in his favourite haunts. He believes very strongly in treaty rights; he would like to shoot a ranger sometime, he once told Moraha jokingly. And she noticed a slight narrowing of his eyes as he said it, as if his mind had also considered the real consequences.

Moraha is convinced that Sitting Wind, if properly raised, could become a strong fighter for the preservation of the old ways, and help bring back the game required for the survival of all Indian people in Canada. This could be his special destiny. It could be why the Wind preserved his life when he was a baby.

When Moraha, Ben, and Sitting Wind returned to Morley about two weeks ago, following the Banff Indian Days, discussions and preparations for their trek were immediately initiated. Three or four other families, all relatives, joined them.

Sitting Wind does not yet know the names of all of his new relatives, but Josiah is his uncle. Many are relatives of Grandpa. In tow behind their wagons they hauled extra pack horses to bring back loads of furs and food. The Stoney trail was barely wide enough for wagons and democrats. Sometimes, there were dead-falls to be removed, horses in harness tossing their heads as they drew up to wait. Grandpa Ben called it the Stoney highway.

The party traveled north from Morley, fording the Ghost River and passing through pastures of the Bar C ranch. Water runs low at this time of year, the hardwood spokes churn easily through clear bubbles. From the Bar C they headed across Sna Tinda (Greasy Plains) and, later in the day, across Little Red Deer River. At the end of a full day's ride they made camp on the Big Red Deer River at their usual campsite, near the crossing. The next day, exhausted from long hours en route, they arrived here, at the Melco Ranch on the James River.

Grandpa eased himself from the wagon and lumbered to the door to talk with Mel Thompson, the rancher.

"How ya doin', Ben? Good seein' ya again!" Mel shook with his right hand while pulling a pipe from between his teeth with the left. "Is there anything I can be doin' for ya?"

Mel had told them to come back again this year for fencing.

Soon Grandpa returned to the wagon, smiling. It was all right to set up their tepees again, and Mel had work for them. The wagons rolled deeper into the ranch lands. Harnesses and saddles were removed from the horses, and any burdened packhorses relieved of gear.

The finest location was a clearing, where the creek bends north. Although Sitting Wind does not know it yet, the elders always camp in this site, the edge of an aspen stand at their backs and tepee doors facing morning sun. Ben would stand in tall grass, eyes encompassing in one slow sweep a far circle of hills, the less distant perimeter of trees, and the creek gurgling close in. Every year he would follow this identical ritual, as if discovering this same secluded haven each time for the first time.

"Right here is a good camping place," he announced, gazing full into Moraha's eyes. She agreed, as did accompanying relatives, listing the benefits of water and sun and protection from wind. For each tepee a tripod of tepee poles was cut, lashed together and erected. Additional poles were brought to lean against each tripod and finally the large canvases hoisted and wrapped around. Soon, small fires were flaring for tea and food, the horses grazing nearby. They have been here two weeks now. Two weeks already.

If only there was another child in the party, Moraha thinks as they proceed in irregular spurts along the trail: one of Sitting Wind's age. It would allow her occasional respite from his questions, and enable her to catch up on chores. She wonders if it is detrimental for a child to be with adults only, for extended periods of time. In the old days there were always children. But this seems to have changed, especially since the residential school was built at Morley. Fewer parents take their children into the wilderness now, preferring to leave them behind in care of the school.

The men should be farther along the fence today. Moraha spies fresh shiny staples among old rusty ones, driven into parched fence-post cracks. And there she notices also a strand of new wire, ends bent into loops through which the old wire has been threaded and twisted.

Little Sitting Wind kicks an empty tobacco tin; which could have been used for staples. His hands are encumbered with the water crock.

Although she was eager to begin Sitting Wind's wilderness education, Moraha had anticipated this year's hunting journey also with some anxiety. The first couple of months would be manageable, while the men were busy every day fencing or whatever else Mel Thompson had for them to do. During this time, her responsibilities would be simply to prepare meals, and this allowed plenty of time also to spend with the child. But this period would be followed by the hunting and trapping season, frosty nights and shortened days requiring hard work at butchering, drying, scraping. She is not a young woman any more. She realizes it will become more demanding to provide for both Ben and young Sitting Wind at the same time.

"It will be better if the child and I return to Morley before the hunting begins," she suggested one night to Ben. "He is too young, and I am the only one to look after him."

"Dry-meat must be made, and hides scraped, and food prepared every day," he replied as a matter of fact. "Who will do the work?"

"Josiah's wife, Alice, and her sister," she replied. "They can help. They will be able to do so for both you and Josiah. That way I can stay in the Morley cabin and have time to teach my grandchild."

Ben said nothing further. He needed time to ponder, to decide quietly.

"There's Grandpa!" Sitting Wind's eyes sparkle as his short legs bounce over uneven terrain. The water crock sways dangerously. Ben is crouched beside a fence-post, one knee sunk into flaking clay, his arm and shoulder straining against a short length of pole, levering wire for tension. His bracing is steadfast. Josiah hammers staples.

The men are happy that food has arrived. Sitting Wind helps find some dry sticks near tall willows, while Moraha erects a pot-hanger over a makeshift fire. Tea is soon made, Moraha mixing dough for fry bread, cross-legged on a small blanket. Pasty filaments cling to her lips as result of licking her fingers. She directs Sitting Wind to bring more sticks.

Ben and Josiah have already assumed relaxed postures in grass near the fire, pulling stalks of dry-meat between their teeth, discussing their hunting supplies and what needs to be done. In polite anticipation, their eyes frequently come to rest on the tea pot, and on the dough oozing slow bubbles in sizzling lard.

Moraha turns the bread over to brown the other side. She brought a tin of jam. When the bread is ready she takes it to them.

"We cannot bring the child on our hunting trip," Ben announces off-handedly. "He can go to Mr. Staley's new school. But you must come with us."

She expected his decision would be that she stay with the hunting party. But the edge in his voice still catches her by surprise: he will not have Sitting Wind along? She senses he has been thinking about it for some time. He called him "the child", indicating more distance, separating himself. Perhaps he has already talked it over with Josiah, and any attempt to break his resolution will be impossible, will merely arouse anger, now that he has committed himself.

"Maybe it will be all right for Sitting Wind to stay as well," she answers cautiously. "I could manage both: look after him and do the hunting and trapping work, too. He will be able to help. I will make him help. It is good education for him to live in the old ways of survival."

She knows she is pleading and it will gain nothing. What she means is that she pities this special child whose destiny is strong, but who is also parentless. She feels personally responsible for him: his mother was, after all, her child, her daughter, and no relation of Ben's.

"Sitting Wind shall go to the residential school. Mr. Pringle is likely to be angered if he fails to attend school. We could be breaking the Queen's law."

Moraha considers his words. She is not convinced that it is true; in fact she rather doubts it. But Mr. Pringle is the government's Indian Agent. She does not wish to be the willful cause of wrongdoing, to have Mr. Pringle report her for breaking the law. There are things Ben knows. She would be blamed, appear foolish if he were proved right.

It is true that others have argued that school is good. Their children remain there all year, in residence night and day. The teachers and their helpers instruct them, feed them, clothe them: everything.

Sitting Wind has returned with additional firewood. She motions that it is enough and offers him a chunk of bannock smeared with jam. Moraha assures herself that he has not heard Ben's words, is ignorant of their discussion.

Reclining now with her own lunch, apart from the men, she ponders the arguments in detail. A young boy, her own grandchild, is awarded a powerful destiny already in the first year of his life. This is unheard of, at such an early age! And now he is in her charge. She is responsible to direct his education. What education will he require in order to fulfil his destiny? Where will he get it? At whiteman's school, where Ben wishes to unload him? Or with her in the wilderness, learning the old ways, and becoming a warrior for Indian rights.

Ben is wrong! She knows he is wrong this time. There are times when his unbending resolve is life-saving, but this time it is sheer stubbornness, and he is wrong.

But in her desire to do the best for Sitting Wind, Moraha feels increasingly confused. The whiteman says that school education is very valuable for the future of Indians. There must be something to it. The evidence is all around: how can anyone even argue against it?

She considers the fire-wagon, its massive power under the hands of a couple of operators feeding it coal and water, and the way it rides an endless snaking of steel tracks without slipping off. Its magic wheels. It has lights inside, she has seen them. And then there are guns used for hunting — every Indian uses them now — and axes and matches and.... Moraha is suddenly taken aback by the catalogue of the whiteman's effect on their life. She considers her dress, the rubber galoshes over her moccasins, felt stetsons, fences, farm machinery, hammers, beads, papers, tobacco, flour, tea, trading posts containing shelves of food. The artifacts, even in her immediate surroundings, seem countless.

And yet, fundamental doubts press her from within. Why do some people insist school education is bad when the whiteman has brought all these benefits? What is it that stands in the way of believing and trusting? Is it the money?

"Money is the root of all evil," McDougall used to say. She never understood what he meant. Surely money is good for buying from the Trading Post the things one needs.

Perhaps it is trust. Yes, that's it, it is trust; she does not trust whiteman very much. Of course, some are good people, such as this rancher Mel, or Mrs. Steeple from Nordegg, or Norman Luxton from Banff. But on the whole, no. Not with the way they have taken the land, and made laws to stop Indians from hunting. Not with the way they are causing Indian people to starve. Not with the way they have gone back on words of promise at Treaty.

School education could have something to do with making white-men untrustworthy. The Treaty was sacred, a sacred promise, to continue as long as the sun shines, the grass grows, and the river flows. Maybe school education makes people greedy. At Treaty, they promised that police would protect Indians; instead they put them in jails. Instead of helping Indians, the government has brought rangers, agents, forestry officers, wardens, inspectors — officials who warn: don't do this, don't do that.

Eva Wildman mentioned only a few weeks ago how kids coming home from school for summer months are different, more like the whiteman — they don't respect the elders as much as they should. They used to help and respect each other: that was the most important thing to learn in the Stoney way of raising children. But school children seem to learn no shame; they become bullheaded. The school should be teaching them respect and manners. Moraha has heard that teachers forbid children to speak Stoney.

"You are wrong!" she bursts out suddenly, unable to contain herself.

Ben and Josiah's conversation freezes.

"He is special! A child of the Wind! Did I marry a man who is so stubborn that he thinks himself above guardian spirits? What kind of man are you, that you care nothing for anyone else?''

Sitting Wind, now fully aware of serious tension, sidles off to prod an ant-hill with a long twig.

Ben fixes cold, unwavering eyes on Moraha.

''It is mine to decide.'' His words come after a long silence. ''I have considered what you think. But I am the one who decides.''

''He could be too young for school.'' She offers one last, weak argument. ''We might better wait till next year when he will be closer to six years old.''

''My mind is made up!'' Ben snaps, anger mounting now in his voice. ''We will discuss this no more! Can't you see there's too much work? Josiah will take him back after the fencing is finished. The day after tomorrow.''

Resigned, Moraha rises and brings the men more tea from the fire. They like sugar in their tea now. Ben is probably right, there is much work to do. Sitting Wind would be bored with no children his age. He will need attention.

She forces herself to think of days that lie ahead. After two weeks of fencing they will receive good money, thirty dollars, maybe. It will buy tea, flour, salt, and things needed for the rest of the trip: which will be in the wilderness, where there are no ranches, no cattle, and no whitemen. Moraha recalls the trips in her younger years when Mary was a baby. There was never any debate at that time. No school. Children came along everywhere mothers went, no matter how young they were.

Her baby, Mary, smiled broadly at Mrs. Steeple of the Nordegg Trading Post. ''How about I trade you a sack of new potatoes for this baby,'' the red-haired woman bantered, cradling the papoose in the crook of her arm. ''I'll even throw in a half pound of sweet chocolate.''

Moraha was shy with her at first, but by then she had become like a sister and she laughed along with her. Sam, Moraha's husband with whom she bore children, was loading fresh supplies onto the pack horse outside. Rain was threatening, and he wanted to travel six miles yet before making camp.

The following day they travelled to Kootenay Plains, her smiling papoose swaying side to side in rhythm with the horse's steady stride, in the blanket between Moraha's shoulder blades.

Sam and his brothers usually camped at the Plains for a couple of weeks to hunt deer. There would be about five tepees in all. Moraha worked alongside other young wives, draping strips of meat to dry over smoky fires, scraping and drying hides, and folding them for tanning later on. How young she was then! And what fun she had with her sisters-in-law, joking and telling stories. One or two men would stay in camp to protect the women and children if a grizzly bear had been bothering the camp at night.

Sam was a wilderness lover, too. After the deer were hunted they would move up into high mountains. He had favourite places for fishing, sheep hunting, and goat hunting. Mountain camps would last for a complete moon cycle, allowing her time to tan hides and make new clothes.

In early November, when most hunting was finished, the men would begin trapping for furs: as soon as snow covered the ground, their thoughts would turn to trapping. Each had his own methods of snaring, and some were expert. When all was done, and snow was becoming deep, they would head home, the pack horses laden with supplies.

Other families and their children would gather at Morley, too, for Christmas. Morley was a good place for wintering because Chinook winds cleared the flats of snow, and provided easy food for the horses. There would be feasting, story telling, church gathering, and singing. Children would play. This is how they grew up. This was how she herself, Moraha Lazyback, had grown up at Hobbema.

It is the only life she knows. It is the way it should be. If Sitting Wind is taken to Morley now, she will not see him again until Christmas.

She instructs her grandchild to get the crock while she scrapes the pan with a ragged end of dry stick. The men are squatted cross-legged in the shade, smoking cigarettes.

This afternoon, back at the tepee, she will finish stitching new moccasins, for Sitting Wind to wear at school.

Morley Residential School
June, 1930

"Fold your hands for grace! Everyone fold hands for grace, now! I'm going to say grace."

Whenever Reverend Staley is present during lunch hour, which he usually is, he takes it upon himself to say grace. He is both Methodist missionary for the Stoney Indians and principal of the Stoney Indian Residential School, which was built under his direction and persuasion only four years ago. The school is an obvious success, with attendance already greater than capacity, and he is proud of it. His authority here is unquestioned, everything under his direct control.

The clergyman's eyes quickly scan four rows of tables — identifying all hands on deck, properly folded, and all chins lowered to chests in proper obedience to the Lord God.

"Dear Father in Heaven, bless this food which we receive from Your merciful hand. In these times when increasing hunger and poverty are all around us, You provide in Your faithfulness everything we need. We thank You from our hearts for helping us learn how to till the soil, and grow crops, and use wisely the foods You have provided as our Great Creator. In Jesus' name. Amen."

When Sitting Wind hears the words, "In Jesus' name," he recognizes the prayer's conclusion. A ragged chorus of student voices pitches in for a final "Amen". Today marks the end of his first year at school, and he now knows well the procedures that follow grace. First those at table number one, the grade one and grade two children, file into the kitchen to receive food, chairs scraping hardwood as they rise. Today's lunch is a scoop of potatoes with gravy, a spoonful of carrots, two slices of bread with butter already smeared on them, and a glass of creamy milk. Mrs. Leopard is Sitting Wind's teacher, but she helps Mrs. Landale serve the food at lunch and supervises the children. She smiles at him as he approaches in his turn; a responding smile spreads involuntarily across his face.

"Very good! That is very good!" she said to him in class today. "But you must be mindful to pronounce 'bank' correctly like in 'frank'. It is not 'bink' like in 'mink' or 'pink'.''

The corners of Mrs. Leopard's mouth pull tight to her ears when she smiles now, just like when she exaggerated the ''ank'' sound, pushing her face at the class in bobbing motions.

Mrs. Leopard's life is entirely absorbed by her job. This work is her life. Ladling food from behind a low counter as the next row springs into line, Mrs. Leopard finds the room exceptionally noisy today, children chattering, some almost yelling. She may have to settle them down if the situation gets out of hand.

Most of the twenty-seven children in her grade one class knew not a word of English when they started last fall. Of course it is difficult for them to understand words and grasp concepts with which they have had no experience as yet. On the other hand, the pictures and concepts do offer an introduction to the real world of progress, to which they will one day be admitted if they are given a sound education.

This is, after all, the primary purpose of a residential school: to prepare these children for a better life, to remove them from the squalor of poverty and heathenism. When Reverend Staley asked her and her husband to come and teach Indian children at the Morley residential school, he strongly emphasized the importance of a combined ministry and education for these children, so that nothing would stand in the way of their successful adaptation to society.

It is a labor of love, a major responsibility that she and her husband took on a few years earlier: to teach these young savages, some of them veritable orphans. First, they must be taught correct English, the foundation for any subsequent progress. This is her chief task with the twenty-seven youngsters enrolled in grade one. And it is worth every ounce of her energy, every minute that she lavishes on it. The need is immense and it is so rewarding to see the progress children make daily. She relishes those rare occasions where she can display their progress. No. Where a student displays his or her own progress. God has clearly endowed them richly with talents, talents that have lain dormant or, one could even say, have been suppressed all these years, by lack of education and civilized living habits. She needs only to provide daily encouragement and direction, and the talents will bear fruit of their own. Perhaps she will one day see some of her students graduate from high school, and have the pleasure of watching them become contributing members of society, as they ought to be.

''Mrs. Leopard!'' One of her grade three students has come to a halt before her and is disrupting the line's progress.

''Yes, Beatrice?''

"Sitting Wind has to go to the bathroom. Is it all right for him to go?"

Sitting Wind, at the age of five, is the youngest student in school. In a way it has been good that Beatrice has adopted him as her responsibility, almost as a younger brother. It finally dawned on the teacher one day before Christmas why the older boys occasionally burst into laughter when the youngster spoke; they had been teaching him uncouth Stoney words, which even he himself did not understand. Beatrice is able to protect him from such profanities. The Stoney girls are responsible, and Beatrice covers for him, protects him when necessary.

"Who, did you say?"

"Sitting Wind."

"Pardon me?"

"I mean Frank, Mrs. Leopard."

"Thank you, Beatrice. That is much better. You know it is impolite to address a peer by anything other than his proper Christian name. Don't forget that.

"Frank needs to go to the bathroom, Mrs. Leopard."

"Thank you. But I think Frank has learned how to inform me of that himself."

Her eyes follow Beatrice to her chair. She is seated beside Sitting Wind, and shortly he turns his face in her direction, a fork heaped with potato arrested halfway to his mouth. She waves with her free hand in encouragement. He turns his head away quickly, hiding the irrepressible smile. She has no doubt that he feels comfortable with her.

That has proven to be the greatest challenge, she muses: gaining and holding parents' and students' trust. So easily do they blame whitemen for their woes. Last year a severe flu spread through the community. At its peak numerous students were bedridden and required medical attention. When one youngster died, parents blamed the school, especially Mr. Staley, for not seeing to the child properly. The ensuing gossip hurt the mission. Set them back.

"Is there something you wish to ask me, Frank?"

Sitting Wind has cut into line and is standing before her, his face upturned behind the counter.

He needs to go desperately, but cannot formulate the whole sentence in English the way he thinks it should sound, smoothly and confidently. They are punished for speaking Stoney at school.

"Go bathroom?" He glances about as he speaks, to see if anyone is taking notice. No one laughs, but the clattering of forks on plates competes for dominance.

"Pardon me, Frank? I can barely hear you."

He swallows noisily and tries again.

"I need to go bathroom."

"Say it correctly. Say, 'Please may I go to the bathroom, Mrs. Leopard'. She has brought her face over the counter, her breath warming his scalp, in an effort to make the interaction more private.

"Please may I go bathroom.... Mrs. Leopard."

"Yes, Frank, you may go. But come back straight away when you are finished."

Sitting Wind pivots quickly and escapes into the hallway, the noise finally shut away behind the heavy door closing at his back. The walls of the hallway are painted in off-white gloss, trimmed with dark shellacked oak. A fat blue fly buzzes along the panes of a large window above a silent radiator. He is too short to peer down over the sill, but the sky above is summer blue. Summer.

A washing machine in the laundry room behind the kitchen drones. Sitting Wind stops briefly to study the water-colour print of a Chinese girl holding a parasol: her lips are thin and determined. Maybe she was mad at someone, he muses. At a bad person, a gruff one such as Mrs. Rich. It may even be that the girl is running away, clasping the bony stem of a large, flimsy mushroom with her thin fingers the colour of milk. True, she vaguely resembles an Indian; but her clothes are different, more like whiteman's clothes, shinier, and with more intricately detailed designs.

"Do you have something to ask me, Frank?" He recalls Mrs. Leopard's matter-of-fact question, her firm eyes. "Frank," she addresses him, always. Such a silly word, when you stop to consider the way it sounds in your ear. Empty of meaning. The whiteman's words are short, sterile. "What is your name?" she once asked with those same eyes. He thought about it, gazing beyond her into the strange hallways of the school that was to become his new home. He thought about Sitting Wind. Grandma told him it was a special name, strong.

"C'mon," she badgered. "Tell me your name."

"Sitting Wind," he managed weakly, and his hands felt naked. There was dirt under his fingernails and warts spreading above his knuckles.

"No." Her voice responded so firmly and immediately that he froze. "That is not your name. I want your real name. Tell me your real name."

Fearing to meet her eyes then, he imagined the icy determination behind the friendly and persuasive facade. What did she want him to say? He knew no other name. Neither Grandma, nor Grandpa, nor

Uncle Joe, no one had ever addressed him by another name. He could not respond. He dared not repeat his name again.

"Frank." She finally broke the long delay. "That is your name. Frank."

She made him repeat it again, and again, and again, until he could pronounce it comfortably. Frank. Frank. Frank.

The machines in the sewing room near the end of the hallway are silent now. His brown pants are there, mixed with all the others, but with his own special initial inked into the waistband. The girls sewed a patch on the seat where it was ripped by the teeter-totter. Mrs. Rich taught them how. The pants will be relabelled for a new student next year.

He has accepted bathrooms as part of his daily routine now. Initially, being not only the youngest child at school but also rather short for his age, he deduced that toilets were wash basins for small children. Beatrice immediately set him straight on that point. He recalls his original consternation at being instructed to commit his number two's to the water in the toilet bowl. Grandma would have scolded him for that. "Water is for drinking! For us, and for the animals!" she would have grumbled. The operation of flushing was disconcerting at first. Magic. He wonders where it goes.

Additional memories begin to return, of the day he first entered the Residential School door. Uncle Josiah carried him on horseback from the Sundre store, all the way back to Morley in one day. After spending one night in Grandpa's house at Chiniki Village, they headed directly to school early in the morning. He waited slightly behind Josiah, proudly wearing the new moccasins Moraha had completed before he was led away from her.

"I am afraid he is too young for school, Josiah. I'm sorry I have to disappoint you." Mr. Staley's chin crumpled as he heavily pursed his bottom lip, insinuating that it was not his fault that the school was funded for only sixty-five students this year, and already had ten more than that. There was simply no more room. Besides, the age for entry was six.

"We are not allowed to take in any child under the age of six, and your boy does not appear to be a day over four." Mr. Staley was firm, but friendly.

"He kind of small for his size," Josiah argued in his best English, which was heavily accented: He kindza shmall for hees size, was the way it sounded. Then, taking Mr. Staley aside for more privacy he said. "He is not mine really; just my cousin, I guess." Josiah meant nephew: the English way of naming relatives confused him. "Hees mother died, and hees granmother looks after him. He tolds me to drops him off here. They in Sundre now, hunting, and hee's got no place to go. Anyway, hee's almost five, I think. Close to six.''

"I really don't know where we would keep him, Josiah. It's impossible," replied the clergyman patiently. ''What is his name?''

Josiah's eyes brightened somewhat. Mr. Staley was interested in the boy's name.

"Youtnah Peewin," he responded instantly.

Mr. Staley's forehead furrowed, and Josiah explained.

"That hees Cree name; in Stoney, Ganutha Ingay: boz ways it means 'Sitting Wind'.''

"No, no," Mr. Staley said with growing concern. "Christian name. Christian name! He must have a Christian name."

Josiah's eyes fell. He had no answer to satisfy the clergyman. It appeared the child must come on the hunting trek after all.

"That's only name I heard. Sitting Wind."

With an air of authority, Mr. Staley summoned Miss Landale and conferred with her. Young Sitting Wind heard them exchange words such as "heathenism" and "orphan". Miss Landale was the one who then took Sitting Wind's small hand and he became the very youngest in the school.

It was like entering a new world. A world apart, inside a large three-storey house, tall like some of the houses he saw during the parade, and full of children and strange activity. Everything was completely foreign to the life he had been leading until then, in log cabins and in tepees. The school had a long stairway like a tunnel; but it was clean, and one could walk up or down without using hands. Down below were voices of kids yelling, playing, having fun. But at the same time it was scary, almost everyone speaking English or, occasionally, Stoney. Sitting Wind understood no English, and his Stoney comprehension was limited.

He arrives at the bathroom door. The sign reads "Boys," and he repeats the word to himself, rounding his lips as Mrs. Leopard does when she enunciates. She always says "Good!" with wide smiling eyes, beckoning vigorous encouragement with her delicate hands as if she were pulling in a hooked fish.

He wears suspenders now, and real pants like the whiteman, with buttons to open and close them. Beatrice told him he may not wear a breech cloth or moccasins any more. The church collects proper clothes for students of the residential schools.

Snaking out of his pants he sits on the toilet and studies the cement floor, grey like stream-side clay, pitted with thousands of minuscule hollows. Black shoes have streaked the floor. The paper is softer than the moss.

Grandma has never been inside the school; he has not been able to show her all these different things yet. What would she say about him? About the school? About his new name?

He watches the flush as he buttons up meticulously. He can reach the mirror when he climbs on the empty horseshoe crate, his face appearing to be cut in two by a crack in the glass. Dan did that, cracked the mirror, the time he was crying and threw the bar soap which smells like berries.

Studying his reflection, Sitting Wind tries to recall his appearance before Mr. McLeary shortened his hair. He imagines braids hanging by his ears, like they used to do. If he neglects to comb his hair one morning, after washing up, Miss Magee sends him back upstairs to finish before he sits down to breakfast.

Finally satisfied, he heads back toward the dining room. They took away the beaded moccasins, and fitted him with real shoes like the whiteman's, with rigid soles and hard square heels. They clap audaciously on the hardwood floors unless he takes care to let them down softly at every step.

Today is the last of the school year, and there will be singing and a special cake because the summer holidays are beginning. Grandma and Grandpa will be coming to take him home: all the parents are coming to pick up their kids, Beatrice explained. Perhaps it will be Uncle Josiah who comes. The cake will be special.

Back at the cafeteria door, he listens at the crack before entering. Mr. Leopard is talking loudly to the students, telling them that after the cake is finished all students may go to out to the playground until their families come for them.

''Don't forget! Be sure that your families have spoken to me or to Reverend Staley before you leave with them.'' He is shouting because the kids are excited, noisy. No one notices as Sitting Wind re-enters, the door closing easily behind him.

The lineup for cake is forming. Beatrice speaks Stoney to him when the teacher is out of range. ''Did you wash your hands?'' she asks him. He likes Beatrice.

''It looks as if they've forgotten about you!'' Mr. Hogarth says it teasingly, as if he has detected Frank's mounting anxiety and wants to reassure him that there is no cause for worry.

How could they have forgotten that today is the last day of school? Everyone was told; Reverend Staley even reminded Grandma two weeks ago when she came to bring him to the Morley cabin for a night.

Sitting Wind grins at the caretaker; he recognizes his teasing. The blue coveralls that Mr. Hogarth is wearing are stained with smears of grease, and his fingernails are etched in black. As he reaches in under the washing machine the side of his face is distorted against the enamel tub, his mouth squishing the words as if they are rabbit-words.

The motor comes free and Mr. Hogarth eases it to the floor with a groan of accomplishment. "There. We have the obstinate beast!"

The motor is black and has wires. Sitting Wind has never seen one before.

After carrying it to the workshop, Mr. Hogarth takes it apart, all the pieces having significance, being cleaned and studied meticulously like elements of a jigsaw puzzle.

"I'd say it will be good for one more year, and then we'll have to get a new one," he mutters casually as Sitting Wind watches, craning to see over his elbow.

Once all the pieces are reassembled, they return it to the laundry room.

No one comes for him. When he climbs upstairs to bed that night the stairwell echoes hollow footfalls. The rooms are empty of laughter and chatter of other students. He sleeps in silence. No one has come for him. No one.

Next morning, Mr. Hogarth comes up to rouse him out of bed. Sitting Wind is already awake, the sunshine burning a shadow trellis on the wall, and robins melodiously signaling through three vent holes in the dust layered storm window.

"Come on, Frank, my boy! Time to get washed up and have breakfast! Your grandma is bound to arrive sometime today, I should think. In the meantime, you can be my helper again!"

Sitting Wind peers through the soiled glass at the landscape.

"I'm up," he responds, sending the friendly caretaker back down the stairs. Yesterday's laundry is flapping easily in the fresh morning air. The view from his third storey window extends almost above the gravel benches that hide Mr. Rodger's Trading Post. Hides Grandma's house too, which is still farther and more to the left, behind where the Union Jack shimmers from its flagpole at the Agency.

He imagines Grandma coming through the cabin door, the hinge squeaking and the door clapping shut behind her. She would be carrying the water pail, going to the creek; and then making ready to bring him home.

Breakfast, in the otherwise deserted school kitchen, consists of bacon with two eggs from the hen house, and some bread that the older students baked. He helps Mr. Hogarth: but still no one comes.

Late in the afternoon, his fears become overwhelming. Maybe they have gone camping without him. Maybe they will not come at all, and he'll somehow have to amuse himself all summer, without even his friends. And what about the Stampede, and Indian Days? The other students said everyone would be there. But not he? He would like to walk over to Grandma's house; someone must be there. But Mr. Hogarth will not allow him.

"You don't look very cheery today, Frank." Miss Landale's voice has just bounced into the kitchen. She is wearing her best coat, with silver buttons. Going to Cochrane, hitching a ride in the buggy with Reverend Staley. Her blue eyes are pitying, but animated with her own summer plans.

"Are you worried because your grandma has not yet come for you?" she asks sympathetically, briefly crouching down to his level. "Don't worry. She'll be here soon. You'll have a good time this summer. Think of all the exciting things you'll be doing." Her young arms have gathered him like a basket full of eggs, and she swirls him around until shy laughter bubbles up.

"See, you'll be just fine. You'll be glad to see them." Letting him down in a descending swoop, her hands slip over his ears as if she were looking into a glass ball.

"You give me a goodbye hug, now. I won't be seeing you for two whole months you know, and I want you to promise that you'll take care of your grandma. You tell her I think she's a very sweet lady."

Sitting Wind hugs her briefly around the neck. She smells like fresh bread. With a small wave of her slender finger tips she slips through the door.

For Sitting Wind, her momentary bright presence accentuates the silence she leaves behind her, and loneliness immediately begins to return. At first it comes slowly like water quietly leaking into empty spaces where before there were voices playing and singing, filling the holes that two days earlier were filled with happy children excited to be returning home. But now the rooms are oppressing and stifling to him. Sitting Wind craves to be in the wilderness with Grandma and Grandpa. Why are they not here to take him, their child, as other parents do? He longs to be outside, to fill his lungs with a deep breath of fresh air.

Making his way down the hallway toward the main exit, he discovers Mrs. Rich in the sewing room. All the desks and chairs are piled against the wall, one on top of the other.

"Well, Frank! How would you like to help me, eh? You can be the sweeper. Would you like to try that once?''

The air is thick, smells dusty. The room feels dark and dingy.

"I think I'll go for a little walk, play outside," he tells her.

"You be careful out there now. Don't go getting into any trouble, you hear?" Mrs. Rich doesn't seem overly appreciative of children. "You stay right by the building."

Suddenly the school feels like prison; the rules are prison rules. Grandma and Grandpa are not coming to set him free, nor is he permitted to leave on his own. Loneliness overwhelms him.

Why does nobody want me? Why do I have to stay here alone? His sluggish feet, making for the door, drag on the hardwood; the walls echo back the scratching, scraping. He needs to cry, to blurt out his pain to someone who would understand; but not the whiteman. He cannot break down in view of the whiteman.

The moment he emerges from the school's front door, the sun wraps him warmly, lovingly, on its gradual descent toward the mountains. It seems to be telling him not to feel sad. "Look, listen, the air is full of your friends, your brothers, your family," it seems to say.

But he cannot respond. He does not listen. Nor does he hear the wind brushing his face, and reassuring him: "I'm watching out for you. Don't feel unhappy."

He can only picture Grandma and Grandpa and Uncle Josiah and all the others in the wilderness, maybe someplace far away, making tea over a small lunch fire and conversing calmly about the berries and the game.

He casts his eyes in the direction of Grandma's house; it is hidden by the crest of hill. The tall fir snag stands motionless, like a hollow skeleton guarding the entrance to a secret landscape, beckoning exploration, promising adventure.

Even the spruce beside it is dwarfed by the immense size of the fir. If only he were a bird, an eagle; he could be perched in top of that tree looking over his domain. Free and powerful. His sharp eye would pick them out, their camp, amid the miles and miles of country all around.

But there's no hope. He is small and powerless, can do nothing to make it happen. Collapsing into a corner of smooth sun-bathed rocks and gleaming white wood siding, Sitting Wind cries softly, the lump in his throat clutching, seeking to free the pain of feeling unloved and abandoned. He cries himself to sleep, the rock holding him.

And sleep offers a soft cushion, like goose down floating in the warm breath of a mother's song. A hand pushes through the down. He becomes aware of it; a soft yet strong hand, brushing feathers away like snow evaporating. The voice becomes manly, authoritative but paternal. It says, "My boy, you shouldn't be unhappy. Don't cry or be lonely. You are going to be a great leader and make everyone else happy."

Suddenly, children are playing and talking in the background somewhere: he can hear them clearly. Grandma is laughing with her hand to her mouth, and Grandpa's cough is deep and rasping.

"Never worry about anything that happens to you," the voice continues. "Whatever happens, it is only because that is the way the Great Spirit wants it. He has determined it."

As he sleeps, his breathing becomes regular: the Wind is protecting him, the sun keeping him warm. Ground squirrels stand on hind legs and whistle, sweet dandelion flowers clasped in fore-paws.

Eventually the sun slips behind mountains that frame the western sky, and Sitting Wind wakes up chilled.

Back inside Mrs. Magee prepares a warm supper of potatoes, beets, and milk.

"Why, your face is disgustingly smeared! Before I serve you anything, I want you to go upstairs and wash up! Use soap, mind you! Behind your ears, too."

The next morning Uncle Josiah is at the door, and Sitting Wind rides with him into summer.

Morley Rodeo
Early Summer, 1934

Uncle Josiah is like a brave and strong chief, nine-year-old Sitting Wind thinks proudly as he peers through elbow-polished corral railings at the action in the chutes. His uncle's face appears tensed with concentration.

It is Stoney Sports Day at Morley, an annual event where bravery and skills are challenged and honed by mean cattle and ornery broncs: an event which confers honour upon those who exhibit the virtues of strength and survival.

Josiah cinches the rope so tight that the horse's spine underneath him jerks spasmodically into a trembling arch, like a bow bent to the limit, straining to let fly.

"Wait 'til I get my legs down!" he hollers in Stoney.

Sitting Wind's heart pulses wildly as he watches. The boys alongside the chute are too eager to release the gate. Their sun bleached cowboy hats with tightly curled brims are dirty grey — dark wet grey around the band where sweat sponges through and holds the dust, flung up from hooves and spurred boots. Their faces are shiny like cooked grease, but they grin widely when they're not clenching teeth or biting a tongue during bursts of concentration.

Josiah spits out his tobacco plug over the railing, a mash of black fibrous tar. Barely misses the young Goodstoney lad who, being duly impressed with the seriousness of the sport, merely lurches back a step and squints his eyes into a tougher, more grown-up expression. Josiah checks his grip one more time, flexing his hand where it jams between the rope and the gritty hide. He is ready.

"Let em go!" he hollers, and compresses his lips tightly in anticipation of both extreme exertion and the penetrating dirt. As he shouts his left hand cocks up as if in salute. A salute which accepts no defeat.

The gate swings open and the bronc shudders briefly. Then, as if suddenly prodded into combat by terrors of death clamped to its back, all muscles contract at once, catapulting the full weight of the bronc like a living earthquake headlong into the rodeo circle.

"Hang on! Hang on!" voices shout from among crowds of by-standers.

The rushes of air feel good on Josiah's face as the maddened animal lurches jaggedly in a boiling tangle of space and hard turf. His hat flies free, away. He will show them he is a real cowboy who isn't thrown easily.

Sitting Wind's heart leaps as he watches the reckless cayuse bouncing up and down like a jackrabbit in tall grass. And Josiah's body clings tight into the parallel gyrations, his arm flinging like a disjointed member and his back jack-knifing in and out like a barn door hinge. His uncle is the world's best bareback rider as far as he is concerned.

"Hang on! Hang on! Make him stand quiet!" he attempts to cheer above the commotion. He can taste victory like sand in his teeth. He wants it. To be part of it, with his uncle.

At every lurch the horse farts and grunts deeply from the lungs, as if dying, being strangled at the belly. Its eyes are like glistening fried eggs somersaulting through a sand storm. Two eggs, stringy bacon, salty horse sweat. Then, with an unexpected twist under and down to the left, Josiah is tossed off the right, arcing to the ground like a sack of dusty onions.

Fingers clamped into a fence-post crevice, his breath arrested, Sitting Wind is poised to take in every element of whatever may follow next. The cloud lifts, drifting. Josiah emerges searching for his hat, as the flurry of cheers, clapping, and shrill catcalls subside. Hanson Bearspaw is the clown again. His face all white-washed, he hobbles around in bright yellow pantaloons. The kids laugh at his antics.

"Mean bugger, dat one. Meanesht bugger I ever rode," Josiah declares off-handedly. He waddles bow-legged in small circles behind the chutes, elbows flexing demonstratively, moving away from too many eyes as if disoriented. It is not quite shock — more disappointment — and he needs to bring it under control now, translate it into reasons, explanatory actions.

He is no beginner. He's on the organizing committee this year with the Chief and several other Stoneys, Claude Brewster, and rancher Ed Rowe.

Ben agrees with him that the bronc appeared to be a tough one. "You rode 'im good though. Rough horse, but you rode 'im good. Stayed on almost right to the end, looks like."

Josiah does not respond to Ben, does not glance at either of them.

Sitting Wind pipes in, "Good ride, Uncle Josiah. I saw you kicking him hard. Were you kicking him hard?"

"I kick the son 'o bish all right. I should 'a kick him lotsh more. Next time I kick him more anyways. Lotsh more," he mutters loudly — in English, to ensure that non-Stoneys take it to heart as well. He is no loser; he is not defeated.

The thought of revenge has brought a smirk across his face: a signal to Ben that Josiah is softening, ready to joke about it.

"My brother made me ride a wild buffalo calf once," he laughs, encouraging. "I was only twelve years old. That's them old days." He taps the lid of his snuff box and offers Josiah a wad. "We were chasing them on racehorse flats near Ozada, where the Bow and Kananaskis Rivers meet, and they ran fast. But we chased them buggers and they jumped right over a snowbank. Except for that one calf; the snow was too deep and it got stuck. My brother says to me 'You're gonna ride that buffalo calf.' But I was scared. I was only twelve. He said, 'C'mon, you want to be a man? Ride that little thing.' He grabbed me and put me on. Told me to hold the long neck hairs. Then he pulled it out of the snow and turned it loose. Damn thing threw me right into the snow. I hardly had any clothes on, but never got sick. Bucked me right off with hardly any clothes on!"

They laugh. Sitting Wind laughs too. He and his buddies have tried bucking some school calves, but Mr. Hogarth becomes angry when they are discovered. A few times he was beat by the calves too. Bucked off. He's a cowboy like Josiah. Like Grandpa was when he was only twelve.

Another Joe, Joe Fox, is the champion this year: he stays on. Some white cowboys call him "The Fox" instead of just Fox. They say it as if they think he is sneaky, dishonest. Maybe it's because they don't like it when he wins.

While the crowd's attention is focussed on another rider, now breaking from the chutes amid shouts and cheers, Ben leads the way toward their tepee, which Grandma has erected nearby. Josiah is hungry and thirsty.

"Maybe some time you can teach me a few tricks about riding cows, Uncle Josiah?"

Young Sitting Wind stretches his stride to match those of his hero, and his tone of voice suggests they are partners.

The boy is cheerful; there is so much challenge and opportunity ahead. The very air in his lungs feels exhilarating. Blue bells are in full bloom on the gravel benches, and a glance reveals the entire valley blossoming a ground-level mist of cerulian blue. Even the generally barren grounds surrounding the residential school buildings, stretched below them along Mnee Thnay's opposite shore, are speckled with colour: velvety brown-eyed susans with floppy necks, white sprays of yarrow. Grandma took some yarrow leaves once, crushed them with her fingers, and told him to stuff them in his nose for his nose bleed. It stopped the bleeding.

"You bet. I'll makes you a champion cowboy," replies Josiah. "Anyways, we'll have lotsa time yet, before de school season starts again."

Sitting Wind pulls his eyes away from the all too familiar school grounds. The moments spent among his family, during summer months, are happier, more fulfilling.

The tepee is hot inside with the sun beating down during the middle of the day. Josiah doesn't like beef jerky much. "Whiteman's meat tays different," he always says. But he always eats some nevertheless, tearing off chunks that he clamps between his molars.

Every week each family is permitted a government ration of beef, flour, salt, and tea. That's because it's the Depression, as Mr. Leopard calls it. He is talking about the hobos, who have been seen on the railroad tracks recently. They are poor like the Indians, have no place to work.

"So you like to be a cowboy, eh?" says Grandpa to Sitting Wind.

Grandma told him he's going to be a great leader, because of his name being "Sitting Wind". And he also had a vision where a hand reached to him and the voice said he would become a great leader, making the people happy. But the concept is vague. Should he be doing something about it? It doesn't strike him as something one prepares for; it just sort of happens when you become older and the people want you, because they respect you. He's used to calling himself Frank now; that's what most everyone else calls him. Only Grandma, she still calls him Sitting Wind, but maybe it's because she is an old woman. It's just as well to be a cowboy in the meantime; people seem to like that too. They clap and shout.

"Yup," he replies. "I want to ride buckin' broncs."

"Well, you better try some calves first, and when you can ride a calf then you try a cow. That's how you start; if you start with the mean ones right away they'll throw you off every time, and after a while you might get scared. You could be hurt.

"It's like being on the Council," he says. Ben serves on the Council with the Indian Agent. It's hard to make decisions sometimes. Not all people like the decisions equally. They can buck like a horse. Every time they have a Council meeting the Agent gives each Council member five dollars. "You need some experience first. They can throw you off easily, even if you make a good decision."

Josiah laughs at the analogy. Sitting Wind snickers, too, but he is not yet old enough to understand.

"Were you a chief, Grandpa?" Being a chief, even a minor chief is considered the greatest honour one can have bestowed. It's something he could brag about to his playmates. "My grandpa was a chief."

"I was a minor chief once. But I didn't like it much, people watching you and waiting for you to make a mistake."

"What is it like to be a chief, Grandpa?"

"A chief has to be friendly and experienced. Wise. He helps the people with everything they need. He helps them with family problems, he counsels marriage problems, and gives people food or money if they are desperate."

Being a cowboy and staying on seems more difficult, and would certainly be much more exciting, Sitting Wind decides.

Morley Residential School
Spring, 1937

"Today I want you to imagine what your life will be like ten years from now."

Mr. Leopard's voice drones monotonously across blank classroom walls.

"There are several of you," he prods them, "like Stanley and Ken, who will be graduating this year. Do you realize what that means, Stanley? It means this is your last year of learning here under my supervision. It means that from this point on, your education — designed to prepare you for the rest of your life — is considered complete, and you must strike out on your own. I want you to imagine yourself ten years in the future, Stanley. What will you be doing with yourself? What will daily life be like?"

Stanley, who is tall and lean, is uncomfortable because he does not have a firm idea of what he will be doing ten years from now. That is a long time away. He could be raising a family, or hunting, or doing something else. He shrugs his shoulders, eyes finding refuge in the humorous cowboy doodles he loves to pencil along the margins of his notebook. Maybe there would be some work around somewhere so he could make some money when he needed it. Whatever happens, he's not one to worry excessively about tomorrow.

"Come now, think about it. Everybody think about it. You need to plan ahead. Planning ahead is the single most important step. For example, no matter what you are going to be doing, you will require money to survive. You need to make your living somehow. That is why I am teaching you about farming and ranching. For your survival.

"How about you, Frank? Suppose you have your little farm all fixed up. You are married and have some kids." His classmates laugh about his being married. "And suddenly you wake up one day realizing you cannot manage without a wagon and a team of horses. Tell us. Where and how are you going to obtain them, huh?"

At the sound of his own name, Sitting Wind has jolted. But to his relief, the teacher has already shifted his animated gaze to another student. Mr. Leopard becomes increasingly excited while talking about the future. So excited that his voice modulates to a higher pitch and embraces additional layers of volume, transforming his whole presentation into one of a missionary. His questions become rhetorical; he answers them himself as if debating with himself. The role of the students seated before him is only to sponge his model energy, to be infected by his show of commitment and enthusiasm for life and progress.

"You see, you would first of all need to plan a trip into Calgary to buy these things. You cannot obtain these necessities near here. Mr. Rodgers does not sell horses and wagons across the counter at the Trading Post, does he? So you would need to go into Calgary to purchase them.

"And then what? How do you determine how much money to pay? Who of you can tell me?"

The adrenalin aroused at being personally addressed subsides again, and Sitting Wind's mind lapses back into the more exciting events which took place this morning.

"Who-o-o-ah! You almost got me!" Earl Wildman, his classmate, and his best friend, jerked back and stumbled towards the barn door, wiping a stream of warm milk from his ear. Sitting Wind had the cow's teat cocked in his fist. He was grinning widely, and poised to squeeze another jet should his buddy approach within range. The wobbly milking stool legs threatened to collapse and send him flailing backward onto the straw- and manure-covered concrete, soupy beneath the next cow.

"I'll tell Jennifer you squeeze good!" Earl taunted him. "She'll like that I know."

"Go ahead. I'm not even interested in her."

Although he is now almost a teenager, Sitting Wind's physique has shown no normal spurt of growth. He remains small, light of bone. But, in his mind, he is all the more challenged — resolved to be strong, brave, grown-up. He will be a leader, an expert cowboy like Uncle Josiah and Grandpa Ben. His peers sense his underdog determination, and enjoy its sheer recklessness.

The barn is located between the school and the river, the shiplap siding painted white, and capped with a red roof, like the Agency and all the other buildings in Morley. Brilliant spring sunshine flooded the entrance near which Earl stood clutching the door-post, out of reach of the milk spray. He kicked a clump of freshly soiled straw at Sitting Wind, aiming at his backside, but suffered immediate regrets as it almost landed in the milk pail. If it had, there would have been serious consequences.

With a whoop and a holler Sitting Wind jumped up, grabbing the bucket of udder disinfectant, and raced into the barnyard. But Earl was faster.

"I will tell you one thing." The teacher's voice cuts through the reverie. "It would be a mistake to go in to Calgary without any idea how much money to bring along, without knowing what is a fair price. If you let the salesman decide, he will assume you have plenty of money and will start by trying to convince you he will need all you have. In other words he will cheat you if you have have not prepared yourself. Before you can go to the city, you must calculate how much money you have, and how much you will need. If you have not enough, you will need to know how to calculate what you must save in addition. That is where the arithmetic comes in, you see. You must be able to count money."

"Hey! What's going on in there!" Mr. Hogarth's irate voice bellowed from behind the granary at their commotion near the barn. The boys jerked to an instant halt and adopted innocent postures when they saw him: legs spread slightly apart, one hand on his hip and the other tipping his hat — allowing fresh air to cool the sweat on his forehead and on his bald pate. He looked like he meant business.

"What do you think you're doing?" he said again.

He could not afford to have horseplay around the farm. Eighteen hundred acres were now operated by the school, with a herd of sixty beef cattle, a dozen milk cows, fifteen horses, and pigs, and chickens. There was much work to be done. In the last few days he'd had to manage without several of the older students: absent for who knows what reasons — rodeo, or branding, or something. He'd be happy to put these two out there working up the spring garden soil, if they'd finished their normal chores.

But the chums declined to answer. Avoiding his gaze, they started to retreat, hoping he would say no more, would ignore them so they would not have to declare their guilt.

"Go finish your milking, Frank!"

He studied their expressions carefully as he delivered his instructions from across the barnyard.

Earl, Frank, Paul, and Stanley are among the older students now, in grades seven and eight, and the older students are charged with the more demanding daily chores such as milking.

"And you, Earl. Come here and help me clean out the oat bin."

That was punishment in itself, since Mr. Woga (which is what the boys call him when he's out of earshot, and is the Stoney word for "grasshopper") is a mean worker. He works you hard until you really sweat.

"It is healthy for you," he says. "Teaches you self respect and discipline. Not a true man was ever born who was afraid of a little hard work, you know."

"And what do you think would result," — Mr. Leopard's voice forces its way once more through Sitting Wind's dazed senses — "if you were to take all your money, every cent you have, and use it for purchasing all the things you required immediately, without saving any of it? That would cause serious problems at home, right? Your wife needs food for the table, and your four children are running around the house on bare feet. They are your responsibility, so you'd better calculate ahead of time how much money you will require for their food and clothing, too."

From the corner of his eye, Sitting Wind notes that some of the teenage students, mouths agape and eyes wide, are mesmerized by the awesome responsibilities and expectations that are being outlined.

"Let's ride some cows later," Earl shouted in Stoney over his shoulder as he sauntered to the granary. "Bert is getting a saddle, and he's gonna bring it."

"When?"

"After supper!"

"Okay."

Sitting Wind is impatient now for the class discussion to be ended, so they can go outside and ride the cows.

"What are you boys saying to each other?" Jock Hogarth said irritably. Although he did not often let on, he could not stand the disadvantage of not being able to understand the Stoney language. "You know the rules. No speaking Stoney when you're at school."

Mr. Hogarth is concerned about the high levels of poverty and unemployment throughout the country. The depression is in full swing. In spite of the national condition, the Residential School has been strengthening steadily over the last decade. Providence has been good to them. For that matter the Depression has served to give more credence to arguments in favour of a residence program on the Indian Reserve, a program dovetailed to education in practical agriculture and ranching skills. Last year, for example, there was enough money left over for the purchase of a new laundry machine. A large J.H. Connor commercial, one that is dependable. This year they managed an addition to the dormitory, enabling still greater capacity. Mr. Staley and the Indian Agent, Dr. Murray, have also secured funds for building a manual training workshop for the older boys. They can even afford to stock it with a complete assortment of required tools.

He teaches them to be organized. The responsibilities of older students, those aged thirteen to sixteen, include milking cows in the morning, cleaning the barns, feeding the various barn animals, and riding over to the McDougall orphanage pasture to herd the cattle down to the spring, and then back to the upper pasture for food. This is a crucial part of their education: knowing how to run a self supporting farm. By simple example and daily repetition, he has taught them how to milk cows, and how to make butter. They now have their own cream and skim milk, and make cheese regularly. He has taught them how to groom horses, how to handle saddles and harnesses, how to ride a wagon, how to raise hogs and cattle, and how to feed them. He has taught them about seeding, planting vegetables, and crops.

When Sitting Wind and the boys finished milking, emptying their pails each time into the large galvanized milk canisters, they cleaned up. With skittish kittens at their feet, they delivered the milk to the kitchen in time for lunch, three abreast with the two loaded canisters between them. Enough to supply the entire school for a day.

"What about if the potatoes don't grow, like what happened last year when it was real dry?" another student, Isaac, wonders out loud. His face is tensed from the weight of every word delivered by the teacher.

Mr. Leopard deflates visibly, the question catching him off-guard. A good point. A genuine concern which has been tossing and turning in his own mind for several years, at supper tables with a spoon of hot custard halfway to his mouth. All this teaching, all this learning and talk about ranching and raising crops — and the Reserve land so reluctant to yield results, especially in the last few years. That is the unfortunate aspect of his work here. When the church and school have accomplished everything that can possibly be accomplished, and have done so exceedingly well, then these young adults are faced with having to try and make it on their own. Where? On land which consists of stones? The "stony reservation": that could cause a chuckle sometimes.

It becomes an economic impossibility. And today, with the foothills' ranchers depending increasingly on itinerant white workers, there is simply no work for the Indians. They must survive on their own — a net closing in on them.

"You must make sure they do not fail. You simply have no choice; be mindful to plant them on time, in good soil, and attend to them throughout the season."

"Should we still go out hunting and trapping, like our parents do and like the Stoneys have always done?" Jordan poses another difficult question. Mr. Leopard, Jock Hogarth, and Mr. Staley have recently started discussing the possibility of establishing a mink farm in the near future, and the prospect appears promising. It could eliminate the need for trapping. But this is still in the future.

"Sure you can. Of course you can. But I would say not for long trips. Just for a day, maybe, as long as someone milks your cow or else she will dry up. And someone must remain at home to feed the chickens and the pigs. See, when you operate a ranch you must look after it at all times or else it cannot succeed. You cannot walk away from it once you have started; all the stock animals are dependant on you for their well-being, and you will harvest rewards only as much as you care for them."

As the presentation winds down, most of the class offer nods of approval. They show Mr. Leopard they are impressed. They feel ready to face the world of adults.

When considering the matter seriously, Sitting Wind also would like to be a rancher, a cowboy, and be settled with a family and house and horse and wagon. The future seems to hold promise for him with the education received from Mr. Leopard.

After supper he and Earl meet Bert, Earl's older brother, at the west end school pasture for some real fun. There is one school cow there which no one has yet been able to ride. They named her "Wildeyes". She always bucks you off.

Bert has the saddle; his father, Dan Wildman, works with the Indian Agent and gets favours. The saddle is an old one, the words "Stoney Agency" pressed into the leather behind the seat.

"Who wants to ride Wildeyes with the saddle?"

Sitting Wind is willing to try something new; he's game. He's always game.

"I'll ride in the saddle!" He nods with determination. "I'm not scared 'a nothin'. She's only an old cow anyway."

Uncle Josiah rode mean broncs and he wasn't scared of them ever, even if they threw him into the dust sometimes. And Grandpa rode the buffalo calf and was thrown off into the snow. You learn to stay on with practice: like being on the Council, as Grandpa had bantered.

The boys laugh.

"All right then," says Bert.

They corner Wildeyes in the pasture against the page wire fence, and rope her by the feet. First Bert's lariat snaps up around one of her rear legs as she steps into it, dodging them indecisively, trying to find an escape route between them. Earl's rope snares one of her front legs as Sitting Wind and Bert battle her; she is thrashing now and bawling.

Once the rope is tied to the fence-post, she settles down, resigned, legs stretched akimbo from corner to corner. They strap on the saddle. Sitting Wind steps back with approval to study it — cinched around the cow's great belly — thinking of how he will now be a real cowboy riding in a genuine saddle. This is unheard of, a saddled cow; he'll be a winner and it will be the talk among the kids tomorrow. It looks like fun. He longs to succeed, to be a cowboy. He could be the one to stay on Wildeyes first.

"I have an idea," Bert says, wiping his scalp with his forearm. "We should tie you in with a rope. Then you'll really stay on."

Sitting Wind recognizes the idea as brilliant. Grandpa always ties ropes around massive loads on the pack horse, and they never fall off. Wobble, but never fall.

With strong half hitches to the stirrups, Bert weaves the rope around Sitting Wind's ankles, bringing them together underneath the cow's belly, and winds it up behind the saddle, tying it securely with complex knots. Then higher still, the rope goes around Sitting Wind's neck, and from there around his waist, to be cinched off around the saddle-horn. For extra security they fasten the shank rope around the saddle-horn, and bind it around his hand. The finishing touch is to pull down his hat tight over his ears, to make certain it doesn't come off.

Standing back to better view their handiwork, Sitting Wind's buddies cannot contain their laughter. Finally they are about to cheat Wildeyes out of her reputation.

Making a sound not unlike his uncle Josiah's triumphant rodeo cry, Sitting Wind shouts, "All right. Let her go."

They relax the lariat ropes, the loops falling open onto the turf. But old Wildeyes continues to stand inert, as though she were bound and strapped to the very ground: a cow harnessed in body splints.

"She probably knows she's beat already!" Sitting Wind says, exultant. "Give her a slap."

The words have barely left his mouth when his face darkens with misgivings. As the cow jerks into motion, he senses wind gathering about his ears, giving instant warning that disaster has wrapped its deceptive web around him.

But the realization comes too late. Wildeyes jumps and twists fiercely underneath him, bawling loudly, and charges for the most distant corner of the pasture. Shortly after, he feels the saddle losing grip on the chestnut-blotched hide, slipping uncomfortably off center, to the left.

The far corner of the pasture slopes down toward the river, but the gate is closed. Wildeyes' direct approach wavers as she nears the gate, causing her to translate her reckless momentum into another flurry of twisters. She gyrates across the trampled mud, water sucking at her hooves, with Sitting Wind rotating in contradictory directions on top of her like a barnyard wind-vane in uncertain air.

She stops briefly, her sides heaving like a huge heart, her red eyes glaring obstinately. Unable to right himself within the restraining ropes, Sitting Wind sticks out like a broken rib, an oblique growth projecting from her side.

"You better not ride her anymore." The boys are panting heavily behind him, lariats swooping through air. But their approach serves only to electrify Wildeyes into action again, Sitting Wind's body slipping lower and lower on her as she jerks and twists. Instinctively he tries to pull his head closer in to her ribs, but the strain of the ropes and the bouncing make it difficult. Her hooves send slop and wet clods by his ears.

By sheer chance her front foot hooks into a sagging loop of body-rope, and her struggling knee-jerks create slack. Blood rushes back into Sitting Wind's rope-pinched arm, strength returning to it. Another volley of aggravated jumps and twists and miraculously Sitting Wind falls suddenly free from the tangle onto the ground — only his left foot remaining noosed; the other ploughing furrows in the mud.

"Rope her! Rope her!" he manages to yell.

But the boys are unable to head her off. Their heads bob and knees pump through the pasty turf in fevered pursuit, but Wildeyes avoids them with equally frenzied determination.

Before Sitting Wind realizes her intent, Wildeyes has switched to a more drastic method of avoidance. She has had enough, and she heads directly for the page-wire fence beside the gate, meaning to clear the top. Dragging like a downed kite at rope's end, Sitting Wind catches glimpses of the approaching fence, but there is no time to think of fear. His foot is burning with pain. The fence repels her, throwing her back, but the posts groan and crack loudly, and staples sing dangerously through the air.

A momentary slack in the line is not enough to release his foot, and almost immediately she tries again for what is now a considerably compressed wire, determined to pull Sitting Wind over the top behind her if necessary. The rope burns along the top, and Sitting Wind meets the fence, his free leg sliding neatly into one of the squares. Pain sears through his body. He hears the sound of more staples singing, and creaking posts, as some thirty feet of wire pop loose.

Wildeyes stops to recover from the exertion, making just enough slack this time for Sitting Wind's foot to fall free.

"Are you all right? Are you okay? Frank!"

The boys' sweat-drenched faces loom over him, moving in and out of focus. They are silhouettes against the glare of the sky, the mountains at the horizon circling round and round behind them, and the mushroom clouds spiraling around him like wool spinning, like pillows absorbing his headlong fall.

"Wait. We'll get you out," they promise, their voices urgent, as they begin unrolling him from a wire prison.

"You okay?" they ask once more, helping him to his feet. The limbs are all mobile; but his eyes are filling with uncontrollable tears of after-shock.

As they prop him up, his arms over their shoulders, one on each side, Sitting Wind cannot resist casting his eyes briefly over to where Wildeyes stands glancing back at them from the other side of the fence. The Agency saddle hangs like a swing from her belly.

"It's harder than it looks," Grandpa had once cautioned. "That's the trouble with ridin'. They don't always have the same idea in mind as you have."

Rabbit Lake
Autumn, 1938

"Did you notice that track crossing our path a short ways back, Cowboy?" Josiah is patronizing, but also serious. He has pulled his horse short and twisted his body half around in the saddle to verify his hunch that Sitting Wind has overlooked the track entirely. The time has come to teach this boy something important.

Keeping kids in Mr. Staley's residential school may have some good to it, but Josiah has noticed one thing for certain: none of the youngsters is learning a thing about survival. For that reason, more than any other, he has serious concerns about the school. So do other Stoney parents and elders.

Look at the whitemen nowadays, all them fellows with whiteman's education wandering along railroad tracks, starved, without any way of making a living. They call it Depression, but as far as Josiah can figure out, it's because they have no knowledge of how to survive in the bush. The worst of it is, it seems that Stoney youth will lose the knowledge too, right now today, if someone does not raise alarm. This whiteman's education is definitely not good enough on its own.

Consider this nephew, Sitting Wind. Thirteen years old already, and he's been at the Residential School for almost ten years. Ten years! But what does he know about the bush? A few more years and he'll be settling down, with a wife. How can he be expected to survive? There is something wrong here, that's clear to Josiah. There is plenty reason to be seriously concerned for today's young people. Josiah's step-mother, Moraha, Sitting Wind's grandma, has pointed to the same problem several times.

Sitting Wind's empty stare signifies that no, he has seen no track.

"That's what you should be paying attention to; don't just sit on your horse looking around here and there as if nothing matters." Josiah speaks sternly to Sitting Wind in Stoney. "You should keep a close watch for signs on the ground, so you'll know what kind of animals are in the vicinity." Josiah has brought his horse around and, with eyes glued to the trail, is backtracking a short distance.

"The tracks we passed are those of a cow moose. A fat one," he says more calmly as their horses hover over half-moon impressions in packed loam. "She will be sitting down on this side of the hill, over there somewhere, below those alders. Stay with me now, and I will teach you how to come close to this animal."

After discharging a stream of tobacco juice over his mount's left flank, Josiah draws a full length of sleeve across his mouth, and decides on his next move.

Last week he finally hauled Sitting Wind aside and broached the subject of survival in the bush; talked about how to hunt and trap. The boy had graduated, and with no school activities to return to, he appeared lost: ready to take a bull by the horns, but with no bull anywhere in sight. It seems to Josiah that when a student finishes this whiteman's education, he doesn't know much other than cow tracks, horse tracks and chicken feathers. In the old days, before whitemen came, kids like Sitting Wind would have learned basic survival skills at a much younger age.

Therefore they set out early this morning from Ben's summer camp at Rabbit Lake, the two of them on horseback, Josiah in the lead.

"You're going to be fourteen this coming winter," he told Sitting Wind. "I think it's about time you learned how to survive in the bush. I'll warn you, this is going to take many days of instruction. But don't worry; when you have learned, I will leave you alone. I'll teach you everything I know: how to come close to an animal, and how to find an animal where it lives during different seasons of the year."

"I had thought about starting a ranch sometime," Sitting Wind confided, in weak self-defense. "I know everything now about running my own place, just as good as a whiteman."

But Josiah merely scanned distant slopes thick with trees, interspersed with small clearings where game animals come to feed on grasses. The kid is still pretty young anyway, he thought. Doesn't know what he's saying.

The ridge they are riding this morning is sparsely wooded with a mix of pine, spruce, and Douglas fir. Down the west side are old aspens widely spread, with scattered roses and buffalo berry bushes near the ground. Down the east slope is a dense cover, mostly of alder.

Josiah leads him a short distance down the trail, well past their sighting of moose tracks. Moose are the most difficult of all game animals to hunt, their huge trumpet ears amplifying even inaudible voices of trees whispering to each other, indicating approaching dangers. They are careful to circle around and bed down where air funnels from different directions and warns them of danger well in advance.

Satisfied with the distance, Josiah dismounts, signalling Sitting Wind to follow suit. In a subdued voice he says, ''We tie our horses here.''

They tie their horses, supple reins looped around branches, low enough so the horses' heads can hang comfortably while waiting, but not so low that they begin feeding and tangle up their feet.

''We'll go a quarter of the distance down the hill from here.'' He whispers sour breath into Sitting Wind's face. ''See those long trees near the bottom? There will be a spring. She will be in that area somewhere.''

Sitting Wind follows stealthily behind, shaded soil cool to his feet through supple moccasin soles. After being clamped into rigid whiteman's shoes for so many years he has almost forgotten how sensuous are moccasins, how immediate their contact with pebbles, twigs, moss. This new pair are like those Grandma made years ago, just before he started school; but the beaded eagles seem larger now, their wings stronger. They are so perfect for hunting.

Bathed for an instant in the rich and pungent aroma of smoked deer-hide clinging to his skin, which has melded with the subtle mildew odours of earth and bush, Sitting Wind almost forgets the objective of the moment. Josiah suddenly motions with his hand, reminding Sitting Wind to be totally quiet, to make no sound at all. They inch in silence down the hill.

Shortly Josiah stops, his mouth pointing at a tangle of dogwood and silverberry shrubs, aspen, and spruce. Sitting Wind's eyes search for a black bulk that should betray her within the vegetation. His eyes find her, standing at the bottom, looking downstream. She is alert, but has not detected them.

Shoot her, Josiah signals soundlessly with a sideways jerk of chin, and gives him room. But Sitting Wind has had little practice, and misses the target.

Josiah's shot follows immediately, as the cow hesitates, trying to interpret. Instantly her knees collapse beneath her large mass. The two hunters scramble to reach her and observe her last breathing: desperate gasps interrupted by fluid gurgles deep within the throat, foam bubbling pink from nostrils. Her eyes roll before the muscle tension relaxes: Spirit letting go, giving up meat for their survival.

As he prepares for butchering, Josiah continues his instructions. ''In the fall season you must hunt enough food for a whole year, making dry-meat and pemmican which won't spoil. These will protect you from hunger later on.'' His relaxed paternal tones betray his new vision of himself as one whose calling it has become to preserve the increasingly threatened old way of life. The entire Indian culture should be preserved because it makes the best sense of all. Better than school education.

"This is the only sure way of survival," he says confidently to Sitting Wind as he draws a knife from his belt. "Even when there is no rain for months, and dust makes dark clouds in the sky, you can always find food like this. You don't need a whiteman's job for that, or any whiteman's education. Simply follow what I teach you."

Sitting Wind finds his own knife and, imitating Josiah's lead, they start at the hooves, peeling away her skin as one large sheet. The women will scrape, soften, and smoke it for clothing items. Next, they cut through the hip joints, and the hind legs come loose. A strong man can carry one at a time over his shoulder, to where his horse waits. Next the front legs, head, and ribs are split away, on each side, from the backbone.

Sitting Wind climbs back up the slope to bring their horses down. All carcass sections are fitted into old potato sacks and slung from the saddles, the weight distributed equally on either side. The hide is folded and tied on top.

"What did you learn at the residential school, anyway?" Josiah asks Sitting Wind suddenly. Sitting Wind shrugs evasively, and Josiah does not press for a immediate response.

He reminds him that the back and rump fats, brisket and ribs will all be cut into quarter-inch strips for making dry-meat. Moraha and Josiah's wife, Alice, will drape them on thin poles exposed to sun and wind, or over fire if there are flies. Two or three days are required for meat to dry. Then it may be eaten at any time, without spoiling. The tongue, sinew pieces, shoulders, hams, and belly pieces will be dried and cooked over a slow fire or on a bed of willow leaves before being pounded into shreds and, impregnated with melted fat, turned into pemmican. Berry pemmican can be made with chokecherries or saskatoons.

Sitting Wind attempts to bring his former school life back into focus. Does Uncle Josiah think the learning was wasted? Year after year wasted? Years which could have been spent with Grandma, Grandpa, and Josiah in tepees, in wilderness? No. It must surely have been worth the sacrifice.

He wonders who is bringing the cattle down to water, now that he is not there anymore. And there is milking to be done, eggs to be gathered, and pigs to be fed: with kitchen scraps at evening, and with fodder each morning. Maybe there were a few potatoes and turnips this year. But carrots not likely. Definitely too dry again for carrots. There is too much rock on their reserve, Mr. Hogarth was always complaining. Nothing can grow well.

"The school was pretty good." He offers a reply at last, one which sounds like an apology. "When you raise cattle and crops for food, you can live that way too. But I guess it's a lot of work."

"That's the trouble with it," Josiah says. "It seems to me this work could be for nothing. It's too risky if the weather is dry or if there's too many cold nights during summer. Once you know how to survive in the true Stoney way then you'll be all right. You'll be better off that way."

Josiah is proud to point out that no part of the animal is wasted. The only things left behind are the intestinal contents. The lungs will be dried and wrapped in intestinal casing; during winter, women will remove the dried lungs, boil them with some meat. They are very tasty. So are the heart, kidneys, livers. The stomach is a delicacy when boiled. The bone marrows also: one throws a bone on the fire — once heated it will crack open easily and its marrow can be drawn out by pulling a willow twig through one end and out the other. Non-muscle parts are always eaten alongside meat.

The brains are sometimes saved for hides, but they are usually eaten. The skull will be split open and the brain taken out in its own casing. The casing around the brain will be tied off and the brain will be dried. During winter parts of it can be removed and boiled with meat. The only non-meat part which will be eaten entirely on its own is the animal's gut. Josiah prefers to boil it or to roast it.

"I may try ranching after a few years," Sitting Wind continues. "I think I can do it after what I've learned. Mr. Hogarth would help me if I get stuck. Or the Indian Agent."

But he is beginning to sense the dilemma of having to throw his chances one way or the other. Ranching would demand all of his attention year round — there would be no hunting, no trapping; none of the old skills would be appropriate to ranching. And Josiah is right. There is proof that whiteman's way of living is not dependable. Proof not only in tattered, penniless hobos, but also in talk of unrest across the great ocean — "rumblings of war on the horizon", he once heard Mr. Staley comment to the Indian Agent. It would be a serious mistake for Indians to abandon traditional ways and depend on whitemen for everything.

He wonders what it would be like to fight in a war. He wonders whether landscapes across the ocean are very different from those of Morley, Rabbit Lake, the mountains.

"The time to kill an animal is when it is fat." Josiah continues to instruct him. "But fat ones are harder to find. That is why we went out today. This cow moose has been eating good food all summer, when everything is green.

"You don't shoot just any animal. Many females will have been feeding their calves during summer; you do not want these. The best ones are dry cows and does, because they will be fat. They are harder to find. The most difficult of all are big bucks. These you must kill before they rut, when they taste good. During rut their meat tastes strong, and they lose their fat.

"Hunting is not merely a game. It challenges you to find those animals which are hard to find: the fattest ones, those which stay in isolated areas during fall or winter and do not move around much. You have to realize these animals will not come to the road; you have to go back into the bush to find them. During spring these fat animals may wander about. But not in the middle of winter. That is how they become fat: they stay put where there is plenty of food in a small area. All animals have a certain time when they are fat and when they are best to eat. That is what you must learn.

"Now we'll have lunch."

Josiah suddenly interrupts himself, satisfied that he has already made substantial progress as an instructor. He extracts a food pouch from the folds of his plaid shirt, ferreting out a small bag of crisp tea leaves, Salada Tea from the trading post. Also sugar and matches. They construct a small fire near a creek, and roast pieces of stomach tripe skewered onto sticks. After a brief search through nearby bushes, Josiah reappears with an empty beef stew can, a makeshift teapot he has hidden on a previous occasion.

"Now, I'll tell you something true about bears, something you must remember when you're out in the bush and encounter a bear." Josiah lectures, as he works, tossing several pinches of tea into the boiling water. "You must never talk against a bear. Never laugh at a bear. A bear knows what you are saying. He will remember what you said or that you laughed."

Flies are circling the pieces of butchered carcass in buzzing arcs and erratic tangents. The pines, sporadically surrounding their picnic site, are less straight and tall than those he has seen elsewhere, unsuitable as tepee poles. An exchange of low flutes and chuckles betrays a fixed-wing approach of grey jays. They sit several branches above, eyes catching glints of sun as they view the scraps of desirable fat strewn about the kill site.

Sitting Wind absorbs everything silently, watching the brown brew simmer under wisps of steam. Around the fire's perimeter, bits of bearberry leaves and juniper shreds curl as they smolder. The flame's heat wafts into his face, smoke burning his eyes. The James River camp comes to mind, bannock bubbling in the fry pan, later to be covered with a reckless smear of sweet red jam; Uncle Josiah's weathered face dripping sweat onto dry fence-posts under his hammer.

"Not everyone eats a bear." His uncle's voice becomes part of the total experience of plant and animal life around the two Indians and their small fire. "There are only a few who know how to prepare it. Have you ever noticed that once a bear is skinned it looks very much like a human? That is why most people do not like to eat a bear. He is like a human.

"Another point to remember: when a bear comes after you, don't run. Just be ready when he approaches on a run. As soon as he leaps in the air at you, shoot, and duck right away. He will pass over top of you because he cannot turn in mid-air as other animals can."

For a few moments they tug at the tripe in silence, savouring the browned soft meat which melts on their tongues.

"What did you learn about plants at school?" Josiah asks after they've eaten for a while, ready now to continue his lessons.

Sitting Wind recalls rows of turnips, and cabbage leaves sculptured by weevils. "Just the vegetables, and the grain like oats for cattle to eat during winter."

"I'll show you how to survive without any crops. You can find all you need right around here. This is the great Spirit's garden which he has made for his people to use for their survival. Use this one and you'll never grow hungry."

After lunch Josiah leads Sitting Wind around their lunch site this way and that. Occasionally he stops and points with his moccasin or picks up a plant for Sitting Wind. "This one here is *wharpaypin* (dock), and when you cook its leaves in a soup they are good to eat. Medicine is made from its root. A similar plant grows up higher in the mountain and is named *wharpaypin tunga* (sheep sorrel) and it tastes a little sour. It is good for thirst on a hot day. During early summer you can find these here *yazobee* (cow parsnips) anywhere. You can cook their stems and then peel off their skins to eat the inside core. They are tasty. Also these *atheebin* (Indian paintbrush) are good to eat if you are stuck. You can eat them raw.

"The best leaves for eating are of *charjay thonthunn* (white willow) which grows near water such as this Rabbit Lake. They do not taste bitter and you can fill up your stomach with new leaves in spring, and feel full and satisfied for a long time.

"I will show you also some roots which are good eating. Learn them carefully, so you will not eat wrong ones and be sick. The most important one is *mommikeeya* (wild carrot, or Hedysarum). You have seen your grandma and other women dig them before summer turns hot. It is not necessary to cook them, simply eat them raw. The grizzly bear likes to eat them also.

"The other one is *seejahnumnun* (wild onion) which grows on dry hill sides facing the sun. And *warchah* (wood lily) in mid-summer. In the foothills you can find *hejeeyahbe bibbin* (wild potato) which you cook and eat during late summer or early fall. But they do not grow right around here."

Aware that the meat must be brought to camp before it becomes spoiled by the day's heat, they lead their horses up the slope at a gradual angle, taking care that the slabs do not shift. Reaching the top, they mount and — side by side — begin ambling back to camp, Josiah recalling a story.

"I'll tell you a story about fishing. See, fishing is another way of survival, another source of food when you are hungry.

"A long time ago there was an old timer who was very hungry for fish. The old guy went out at Kananaskis Lakes in early morning. He took a few long hairs from his horse's tail and brought some meat for bait. He braided the hair to make a line and tied meat to its end. Then, finding a place where a creek enters the lake, he sat down and fastened the line to a long stick. In no time at all, a large trout grabbed the meat. As soon as it realized that there was a horse hair attached, the fish tried to get rid of the bait by letting it out through its gill. The old man laughed out loud at the fish, and pulled it out of the water. This was how he always caught his fish: he would hook them behind the gills this way."

"How is it that none of our people catch fish nowadays?" Sitting Wind asks. "I've never heard you or Grandma or anyone talk about catching fish."

"There are few lakes now where we are allowed. The whitemen made them into Parks and have forbidden us Indians to fish in our usual manner. That's why few people are interested in fishing. But in the old days, we Stoneys caught fish every spring. Even the Kootenays used to come through the mountains and fish with us at Spray Lake and Kananaskis Lakes."

"And they caught fish with horsehairs?" Sitting Wind asks in disbelief.

"No, no," he replies, more seriously. "That was only a humorous tale. The fishing was mostly with nets and with spears, and sometimes with hooks made from a leg bone of lynx. I will show you one time how to make such hooks. Spears' heads were made with antler, small reverse barbs cut into them, and the thin heads bound to long shafts. It is possible to spear fish in creeks."

Sitting Wind is entranced by the stories and the instructions. It seems too soon when they arrive at camp, the women taking charge of the meat, beaming. The youth and his uncle retire to a clearing where Grandpa Ben joins them.

"There's something I want to say as well," says Ben, after Josiah and Sitting Wind have recounted the events of the hunt. He offers Josiah and Sitting Wind his opened tin of chewing tobacco. Sitting Wind stuffs a small wad behind his lower lip and settles into a relaxed position. It has been a long day and he has much to learn. It will take years of learning: not so much remembering, but practising. Understanding the sense of what elders teach, with respect to seasonal rhythms and whims, and cycles of different animals and plants: each making its own contribution to the whole.

The old man carefully brushes stray twigs from the square of canvas he has brought to sit on. His movements have become more deliberate, slower. He complains of occasional pain in his chest, especially after heavy lifting. Briefly he studies Sitting Wind's face, approvingly.

"It makes me happy that Josiah is now teaching you the old way of life," he begins, thoughtfully. "It is good to learn survival. And your Grandma, too: it makes her happy. All day she has been happy.

"I'm becoming an old man now, and one day I'll pass on as old people do. And you are becoming a young man now. At your age you begin to understand things, how a man takes care of those who depend on him for food and warmth. At your age the mind becomes strong, because you have learned how to make the right choices when a decision must be made affecting those in a group for whom you are responsible. That's why I want to give you some instruction, too. Some wisdom.

"Now, I can understand that you may have no memories of your mother, the one who gave you birth. Even I hardly knew her, because it was before your grandma became my wife. You know that your father, John Morin, is a Cree who has continued to live in Hobbema with your older brothers and sisters. Although these people are your family, you hardly know them.

"I don't want you to worry about your family, even after I die. When you become a man you treat everyone as your family, as long as they respect you. Moraha, your grandma, has raised you as a

Stoney; for that reason you should consider Stoneys to be your closest family. You are a Stoney most of all. When your grandma brought you from Hobbema as a young boy, I asked the Stoney chief and council for permission to raise you here as a Stoney. They approved, and ever since then you have been a Stoney.

"This does not mean that you should ignore your father and brothers. You may wish to visit them occasionally, and get to know them. It's up to you.

"As far as your future is concerned, I have something to say about that as well. What I am going to say about your future is what your grandma, Moraha, has related to me over the years. Some of it you already know.

"The year after your birth, you almost died. But a great medicine man whose name was Mountain Walker, called upon his powerful Spirits, and you were healed by the Wind. During that same moment you received your true name, Sitting Wind, and the chant which you would be able to use throughout the rest of your life to call upon the help of the great Wind Spirit. He said you would be a great leader with the Wind's help.

"Moraha was present when you received your name. She heard Mountain Walker sing the powerful chant which is yours alone. She heard your mother, Mary, repeat the chant several times over after the healer departed.

"But, although she has tried many times, she has yet been unable to recall precisely this chant given you to call upon the Wind." Ben moves his face closer to that of the youth, who is now listening intently. His voice is reduced to an urgent whisper: "You are the only other person living today who was present at that naming ceremony, whose tiny ears heard this chant — and you must make a great effort to recall it."

Sitting Wind remains silent, transfixed with the weight of Grandpa's words. Suddenly he feels the future hovering over him, like Mr. Leopard hovering over students seated mute in cramped pedestal desks, warning of dangers and pitfalls resulting from poor planning.

Will the Wind Spirit remove all threats that may lurk along the path? Would it be possible for him to simply place all trust in the Wind? The thought is awesome.

"The song has never come to my mind," Sitting Wind confesses without raising his eyes.

"That may be true," Ben replies. "But let me warn you that the most important messages from Spirits are relayed in dreams and in visions. Take my words to heart, son. Pray for dreams and for visions.

Pray for your song that you may find power in your future. That's all I have to say."

The men shift to more relaxed positions. Josiah says lightly, "You can never tell how it turns out. You could even be a chief someday, and fight for Indian Rights as your grandma always says you will."

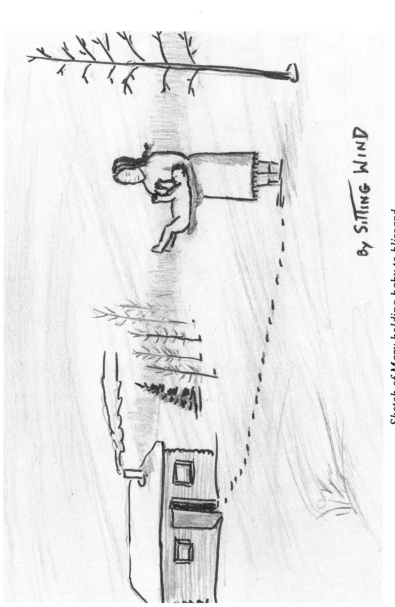

By SITTING WIND

Sketch of Mary holding baby to blizzard

BY SITTING WIND

Sketch of brave's camp by moonlight

Ben Kaquitts and Moraha pose in front of Ben's tepee at Banff Indian Days

Stoney children being photographed by tourists at Banff Indian Days

Stoney children at camp

Row of tepees at Banff Indian Days

Indian parade on Banff Avenue bridge

Parade terminus: Banff Springs Hotel courtyard

Child on travois at Banff Indian Days

The road from Banff to Morley was of gravel.

View of Morley

Agency Buildings, Morley

Morley Trading Post

Setting up camp

Morley Residential School and students

Camp at Morley rodeo

Morley Rodeo

Sweat lodge frame

*Ben Kaquitts demonstrates use of the bow and arrow
at Banff Indian Days*

Moraha

Calgary
August, 1943

"Okay you guys! It's time to hit town and celebrate! Whoopee!"

The exuberant cry reaches Sitting Wind through the open doorway of their sleeping quarters, where he is seated on his own bunk bed: one of twenty or more beds arranged neatly in rows. It is Julian who has called out, a nineteen year old brush-cut with a chapped face. He enlisted only yesterday, the same day as Joe Poucette.

"Where'll we go, man?" responds Barney, four beds over from Sitting Wind's.

The ceiling is bare, and thin plywood walls echo their voices as if they were inside an empty grain bin.

"Hey guys! You comin' along for a drink?" Julian has framed his head momentarily in their doorway now, a jubilant grin spread across his pug-nosed face.

"Where to?" replies Barney.

"I'll find out!" he calls back, already leaping to the next bunkhouse.

Julian likes to have a good time, likes to organize and mobilize the gang. Sitting Wind can now hear him faintly through an open window above, a more subdued and distant voice, flattened in the thick air of dusk outside.

".... Ah... Corporal Hanson, Sir." He must be talking to the short soldier who has hollow bloodshot eyes, near the mess hall. "Sir. Seeing as we're free tonight to do what we wish, me 'n the boys we're thinking of findin' a little pub somewhere for a couple of beers. To celebrate our joinin' the army, you know. Perhaps you could suggest...."

"Just starting, eh? Look right over there. We've got our own ...."

Sitting Wind folds his pants carefully, making sure the pleats have not become misaligned, wandered into the flat ironed wool. This is the good set, they had been instructed; for formal occasions or for going out into public. The clothes fit easily into the large duffle bag, also issued.

The bunkhouses are now filled to capacity at Mewata Stadium, cramped. But they will be here only for another week, they've been told, and then they'll be straight off to Camrose to commence training.

"Looks like everybody's going for a beer," he says to Joe.

Joe Poucette is his cousin from Morley, lean and energetic. Sitting Wind bumped into him downtown.

"Hey, *mayshin*!" The familiar greeting words were shouted from across the pavement, competing with the rumblings of a passing streetcar. Sitting Wind was surprised to hear a Stoney voice amid the traffic sounds far from his reserve. He crossed dangerously, urgently. "Hey cousin, I was searching all over for you." His face glowed as he jealously studied Sitting Wind's new attire from bottom to top. "You look real good in a uniform."

"You can join, too," Sitting Wind said hesitantly. A friend, a link with Morley, would take the sting out of being alone as an Indian among all these whites, on a journey which will end who knows where. "At the recruiting office. As long as you're eighteen. In fact I'm only seventeen; they let me in because they need us Indians real bad."

The recruiting officer had perused the papers and remarked, "A Stoney, eh? I'll be damned! We can certainly use more of the likes of you!" The sensation of his services being valued by a whiteman, by anyone, of making a contribution to an important cause, had warmed him.

"I was there already, yesterday. That's why I need your help. They said you have to come and sign me in." It was because of his bad knee. Sitting Wind had to sign him in on account of his bad knee.

"We should go with them. I could use a beer," Joe adds tentatively.

The idea makes Sitting Wind uneasy, drinking wide open in a public place with whitemen present. People appear official here. There are uniforms. He and Joe are Indians and could easily be singled out, accused. Police officers, wardens, agents — officials have always forbidden alcohol to Indians. It would be better if no one observed them drinking. It's illegal on the reserve, and he would not want to make Grandma suffer the embarrassment if he were charged. They are used to drinking secretly, buddies getting together in the bush.

"We might get into trouble." He offers the statement half as a question. His eyes are caressing his new boots, glazed with black polish. They were instructed to brush them thoroughly, in the cracks, too: like RCMP boots he has seen at the Stampede or at Banff Indian Days. "I don't like anybody to think I'm just a bum or something, so I might as well stay here."

Joe seems disappointed.

"You guys coming?" Barney lurches suddenly from his bed.

"We were wondering whether it's okay for us — Indians — to come too."

"Of course it is." Barney's tone is matter-of-fact.

But Sitting Wind and Joe stay by their beds, uncertain.

"Hey, c'mon, Frank." Barney turns to face them full front, genuinely concerned. "You're a soldier now. A real Canadian."

Sitting Wind is tempted. Maybe it really is different now he's in the army; maybe he's more like a whiteman, to be treated no differently.

"It's okay since you're serving your country. The evening is yours! You can do whatever you like."

"I guess we might as well come for fun anyway," Joe concedes, not too reluctantly. His eyes skim across Sitting Wind's, quickly, to ensure no absolute resistance, and they follow Barney out into warm air.

The western sky is light-green on the horizon, but deepening to dark purple and black overhead. A steep bank of the river hides all but a raw edge of mountains. They now seem far away to Sitting Wind. But the river is Mnee Thnay, and its black silent waters have passed through the distant spread of his reserve.

He hasn't informed Grandma. She does not yet know he has joined the army, unless Earl has mentioned it to someone. It's just as well he doesn't make a splash of it at Morley. The elders are not supportive of the war, McDougall having warned them repeatedly never to fight any more. "It will be against Treaty promises. It could destroy the Treaty," they mutter.

"A jolly good pub, this one," someone says as they clamber up two-by-ten steps into the interior.

It is crowded and dingy. A donkey-eared poster at the entrance depicts the Fuhrer, and is captioned "Nail Hitler." Dim lights are pasted to enamel walls jutting upright between sheets of glowing sky which unroll behind thin, mutton-barred windows. Bare bulbs hang from a low ceiling. The room is crowded with soldiers sitting at small circular tables, several slumped into benign reverie, but most engaged in animated conversation or laughter.

The Herald headline suspended between a pair of hands, leaning on a second table, reads "Canadian Troops in Italy's Mountains". The man studying the columns of black print is wearing his good uniform, with stripes on the shoulder. His short wavy hair is tight to his scalp, with a razor-even part. His tailored cigarette juts straight out from between index and middle fingers, smoke climbing up his knuckles, moving over skin slowly like rain clouds clinging to spring cliffs.

A couple of waiters are bustling, round trays with drinks perched on their shoulders, near their ears, stopping here and there to take orders or exchange friendly banter.

"Over here, fellows!" The call emanates from a couple of recruits from Number 53 Platoon. Julian and some others are already there: a few tables, covered with glasses and ashtrays, have been pulled together.

Two middle-aged males seated at another table, to Sitting Wind's left, have removed themselves from the laughter and hubbub. Their conversation is heavy, albeit slurred. He glimpses a prominent boil on the right side of a potato chin, and globular earlobes. They could be employed in the mess hall, or the laundry perhaps.

"A lot a dem Poles," argues the one with the boil, "Dem's like Germans, I'm tellin' ya. Dat's de truth. I know 'cause I come from dat place once. Dey might look at you like some friend, y'know, but if ya don't watch it dey can shoot ya in de back next sing ya know. You won't even know what got ya. Why d'ya think Hitler overrun dem so easy? Huh? Oh, I know. I know. It's because most of dem jus' fall in line behind dem troops when dey come into dat country. Dey only want dose Jews dat's all. Sneakin' cowards dem. I'd love to be on de line over dere and get my hands on a few of dem hunkies. Dem stupid buggers won't accept me dat's all."

Out of a corner of his eye Sitting Wind watches as the man's misted brew, wrapped in his bulbous hand, is lifted to his drooling lips. There are different whitemen, he thinks to himself. Just like there are different Indian tribes.

"I heard they're still rounding up more of them Japs, too." The man's accomplice leans back heavily in a round-backed chair, causing it to creak like an old tree. "Poor buggers. I was sleeping with some of them in a relief camp at Crowsnest. Good guys, too. Nothin' wrong with them at all ...."

"Same for you, Sir?" The waiter has arrived at his table, brimming tumblers on his tray. His waist apron is marked with yellow and brown beer stains.

The others have ordered draft, Calgary Ale. Joe does, too; there is not much selection. All their eyes are on him. Sitting Wind will have the same.

"Make it two," he says.

"So. What do you think of this, Reg baby! If only your mama could see you now, eh? Did you phone her yet, to tell her you'll be home for the weekend?"

Reginald smiles perpetually, and this grates Julian. He wonders how they let kids like him through the door. But Reginald is nice. He politely grins in response, replying that his family is laying out a special dinner on Sunday.

The boys are shaking salt into their beer.

"Try it!" they encourage Joe, who is studying the white powder through glass, "It prevents hangovers."

Sitting Wind tries it too. After a couple of swallows he believes it, laughing that the beer tastes better this way. The Agency used to provide salt with the food rations during the Depression: he remembers Grandma bending forward, poised with the bag over the inside of a fresh deer hide, her profiled face creased and weathered, serene.

He has prayed for his song. Many times he prayed to learn his special song again. But the dream or vision has not come to him as yet. Not that he has given up. Oh, no. "Don't stop trying!" Grandpa admonished him before his death. Perhaps someday. Suddenly. Out of the blue. But his army buddies wouldn't understand that. They're different as far as that's concerned.

"Hey, you over there. Hey, you Indians!" A man casts seductively low tones in Sitting Wind's direction. He failed to notice him there earlier, doesn't know him, this thin hobo with a few drinks priming his bloodstream. His hair clings, sweaty, brown, molded with a hat ring, his uniform draped loosely over a bony frame. His beret dangles from the corner of his chair.

"What the hell!" the hobo laughs. "Looks like you're in the army, eh? Gonna do a little fightin' for your country?" His grin reveals brown teeth; he is stubbing the pinched end of his wet roll-your-own into the center of an ashtray among the previously smoked stubs: a small gathering of paper cripples.

Sitting Wind turns back to his drink, ignoring him. Joe's eyes are focussed across the room studying the bar, the beer taps, the mirrors. Hobos used to cross the reserve every day a few years back, on the CPR: oily rags flapping from the train cars. Usually a good bunch, though, some of them farmers and ranchers whose lands had stopped giving food — like the reserve lands had — or whose cattle and hopes had dried up.

"If they were Indians like you and me," Uncle Josiah said as they watched a train smoke by, "they would know how to survive with no money, not even a cent." Josiah taught him everything about survival. Maybe that's why the recruiter said, "We need more of them Indians." That's what he said, "More of them Indians."

Hunting and trapping were fun, Sitting Wind soon discovered, but they were largely fall and winter occupations. And, since one does require money to buy other things like tobacco and clothes, one may as well try to get a job during other seasons. With ranching, at least, you could make a living: make money.

Last year he worked with the Edge brothers: Dave, Harry, and Norman Edge. Near Cochrane. He did stooking, threshing, and also ran a threshing machine and drove the tractor for them.

In fact, he was working right there a couple of weeks ago when he decided to join up. The harvest this fall continued late into the season. Pete Labelle was also working there with a few other Stoneys, but he himself was first. Stooking was all right: putting up stooks, tying them in the middle, placing five or six together to keep them dry for threshing.

What he really needs, though, is his own land, where he can start his own ranch.

The hobo has again rolled his eyes upward, snickering softly. "C'mon. Let's see yer tomahawk, huh? Why don't you show it to us, give us a little demonstration? Liven up the scenery a bit in here." His laughter rolls like wheels on gravel. "No offence, friend. Really, I mean it; that Ottawa government must be really gettin' desperate, takin' the likes of you and me I'm thinkin'. You should ask 'em to fit ya out with a bow and arrows. Would look real good on you!"

Sitting Wind sucks at his drink: ignoring.

It was after a long day in the field, in late afternoon when yellow trainer planes came swooping high overhead. Hit him like a flash: what the hell am I doing here? I could be joining them, be where the action is. Why not? They were advertising for young guys of his age.

The following Saturday was payday, and the harvest was finished anyway. It was snowing softly in the mountains. He had heard that veterans were offered free land. The next morning he was in Calgary. They examined him all over, said he was fine, that he could join. He signed up immediately.

"You bettah go piss up a rope. You mind yuh mannehs!"

It's Owen, a negro half-breed; his father is a blacksmith at Nanton. He knows Johnny Lefthand and several other Eden Valley Stoney cowboys. Owen has jumped up and grabbed the hobo by the shirt, wrenching his soggy carcass out of the chair. The bar is suddenly silent, all attention focussing on the beginnings of a fight. Someone hoots encouragement. Nothing like a few knocks for entertainment between drinks.

"He's in uniform, ain't he? Canadians is Canadians, man. You juz give dem yore respect, or I'll have to knock some into yah. See?"

"All right, all right, all right, all right. Don't get yourself in a huff. Just makin a little fun. I wasn't talking to you, anyway."

"They's my buddies, man. Anybody be pickin' on my buddies, then they be pickin' on me, too. Don't forget it."

Owen has relinquished his hold, tossing the hobo back into his chair like mouldy baggage. As he returns to his own seat, the hobo repeats under his breath, "Never knew there was any harm in a little fun."

Sitting Wind makes a move to get up. Why should someone be defending him? He's been in fights before. He can handle himself. He has seen pictures of Joe Louis knocking out his opponents in the ring. He thinks of King Kong, of Sitting Bull. Sitting Wind may be short, but he'll never turn his back on anyone.

"Just ignore the son of a bitch, Franky," his friends smirk at him. "He's drunk out of his senses."

Sitting Wind's glasses are empty. He might as well have a couple more, since they're free: on the house, all night.

They used to go and drink with Stoney buddies occasionally. Some of them would obtain beer from Cochrane and stash it in a bush somewhere, spreading word to a few close friends. It would be after a payday, with no one around to see or hear them singing ancestral Indian drumming songs and having fun. Some of the strangeness of drinking openly is beginning to fade tonight. He is clearly among friends here.

The boys are laughing.

"All right, get this one." Barney is speaking, the others' heads bent toward him as conspirators. "There's this skinny guy and this fat girl, right? He's driving her back home after a date. Anyway he wants to screw her, right? Because he's never tried it before, rolling in fat. He's thinking of it hanging like pig bellies from her sides, huge jelly wallows spilling over her chest. Anyways, he takes her up a hill above Sunnyside, overlooking the city at night, and he says 'You wanna spoon?' She says, 'Spoon? What do I need a spoon for?' He says, 'Hey, honey, you know what I mean: spoon, you know, spoon?' She doesn't get it, right? So she says, 'Sure, you got one?' He says, 'Right here and ready any time,' and promptly pulls out his scrawny stick."

The recruits are nose to nose, nodding with tense smiles after every phrase to encourage the punch line. Sitting Wind has wedged himself into the circle, playing along.

Barney continues, "So she looks at it kind of puzzled like for a minute. Then she cracks up, right? Really cracks up, and says to him 'That's not a spoon! Looks more like a toothpick!'"

They explode backwards with laughter, Sitting Wind sucking more beer, Joe laughing too.

"I suppose you know why we are called Indians?" Sitting Wind cuts in. He once heard this joke in Cochrane and this would be a good time to tell it. All eyes turn to him, waiting.

"You see, it's because of Columbus. He was going around in his boat lookin' for India. Traveling on the ocean up and down, this way and that, searching." Sitting Wind's hands make wavelets through the air, just as Grandpa used to do when telling stories around the tepee fire. "And when he finally landed someplace he saw a bunch of strange people there and he told his crew, 'Hey! I think we've found this land we've been looking for all these years, this land called India. And see here! Here we have some Indians, coming to greet us!'"

Sitting Wind beams around their table. The story is good so far; they are watching him, laughing a little, searching his expression for confirmation of the joke's completion.

"Anyway," he continues after savouring a pause and a swallow of beer. "Ever since the day when Columbus landed, we Indians have always been glad about one thing which is this: that he wasn't lookin' for Turkey."

The group explodes again. "All right! All right!" Julian is slapping him on the back. They order more beer, elbows hinged to glasses. White teeth and sparkling eyes. He is one of the group. They are no different from anyone, Sitting Wind thinks: all people are more or less the same inside.

The hobo remains at the other table, not with them.

Later, after a lull of conversation, Owen the half-breed nudges his arm, "How come you joined, Frank?"

Sitting Wind tilts his glass up, his eyes relaxed, the room a warm blur. He ponders the question. Eleven years at the residential school. It was good. He survived at least, and it was a pretty decent way to live, good food and friends and teachers. But thereafter, not much to do. The ranchers were all hiring white labour now; there was not much money around to buy things. Even when he did find a job, helping with haying or something, they would pay him maybe fifty cents a day plus a meal. Pay him on Saturdays. The old Stoney ways, they're good for survival when nothing else is able to secure your needs. But many whitemen now occupy the trapping leases.

And still there's been no dream, no vision from the Wind Spirit.

He wouldn't mind setting up his own ranch. That's what he would really like. "You must plan every detail ahead of time," Mr Leopard always emphasized. "You will require money for your horse and wagon, and to provide for your wife and children."

He might as well do something. The army gives land to veterans, better than the Morley land, someone told him. He has heard it will include everything he could possibly require. "All you have to do is move right in and start working!" Meanwhile, the army provides for all his needs: a couple of uniforms, a coat, bed and meals, and a dollar thirty a day on top of that.

"Oh, I guess I just felt like it. It looked like fun."

At the recruiting office, the man had sergeant stripes, and wore round wire glasses.

"I'm pretty proud to be helping out!" he had told the recruiting officer. He passed the tests. They took him.

He scans the circle of numbered faces; the boys are waiting for further explanation.

"Well, of course, I kinda like to fight, too," he adds. "Besides, I've heard that Hitler could start fighting us right here in Canada. I'll be able to help out, protecting our land." He downs a glassful and rolls a manly burp off his tongue.

"Hey waiter! Another round for these soldier boys!" someone shouts.

"I don't give a goddam about Hitler," pipes up Randy. "Not for Mussolini either, for that matter, or Chamberlain, or Mackenzie King, or any of those round-faced politicians. Do you think they know about you or me? They don't know you or me or anybody. We're just numbers, nothing more. What I'm after is adventure, that's what I'm after. Good goddam adventure. Gettin' out of the house, savin' a little money, and havin' a good time doin' it too. I wanna screw them Germans. With my own gun, blow holes through them one after the other all over the battle fields. Strangle them into submission."

"You're right about politicians," the hobo mutters, having pulled himself up to join the serious talk. "This Aberhart sure didn't help us like he promised. Guaranteed twenty five bucks a month 'social dividend'. And what did we get once he got in? More relief camps. 'We mean business,' he was tellin' everybody. That was his campaign line. 'We mean business'. Everybody just heard it wrong, got the wrong idea thinkin' he meant to solve our problems. The whole goddam province is his 'business', the way I see it. What this country needs is an enema." He drags on his pinched cigarette stub, brown-stained, and gazes around the table, awaiting a laughter which does not come.

If only he could see for himself a clear road ahead, Sitting Wind thinks. A clear road of survival that he could follow, with chin up off his chest, with confidence, so that he would not feel submerged.

Calgary
August, 1944

Flexing his hand muscles under a tight wrap of tape, Sitting Wind wonders what his opponent, Curly McMann, is like. He has heard people say this will be the tough one, the fight which could reverse his own steady rise to the top.

Bruno, his balding whiteman manager — who is also middle-aged, short, and was once a featherweight champ — is scurrying furtively, checking, eyeing, hesitating, as if making ready for a violent Chinook. Maybe Bruno's worry is a sign that Sitting Wind has taken on too much, that he shouldn't be attempting this fight, which is tonight's main attraction.

"How do they feel, boy?" Bruno forces enthusiasm into his voice. "Put your gloves on and warm the bag with a few rounds while we wait."

Sitting Wind flexes the muscles of his arms and shoulders and lets loose a volley of jabs on the dead canvas. At eighteen he's in prime condition. He has never felt stronger.

Although physically sound and at ease, his mental resolve has become less clear. His original decision to join the army had come easily. With a lack-lustre future in hunting and trapping, and the uncertain prospect of survival by ranching, what could inspire a greater sense of direction and purpose than becoming one of the boys in uniform? Lately, however, alluring as the fun and adventure were at the start, he has been entertaining more troubling questions, questions which he has until now, ignored. What lies beyond the excitement of this moment? What lies in store in the real war? What will happen after the war?

Before being transferred to Currie Barracks from their main training base at Camrose, he and Joe never considered too seriously the dangers of war. But now that they are soon to be shipped overseas, his thoughts have begun to dwell more frequently on what may lie ahead of them. Until now, being in the army has proved exciting, a sequence of events even more dramatic than what they dared conjecture together over beer and cigarettes at the end of long exhausting days of running with loaded packs, parading with rifles, and endless target practice. The evening hours were best, when they became a closely bonded team, laughing frequently, embellishing others' stories to make them sound more thrilling, and more dangerous.

With Currie Barracks a last step before the trip overseas, there is tension in the air, a sense of growing unease. Matters are more serious, provoke more thought. Life would seem too trivial, it occurred to Sitting Wind recently, should it be relinquished merely for adventure or fun. There should be more substantial cause.

It became a subject of conversation with his cousin, Joe. The true rationale, they agreed solemnly one night, their heads laid back on pillows and talking softly into the dark, should one day be explained to the people back home. The real purpose for fighting was to protect Stoney lands, to ensure that Germans would not bulldoze their way over Canada and take away the Indian lands.

"If one of us should die," Joe mused, "It will be first of all for Stoney people: so they can remain safe on their reserve, and gain more power to preserve Treaty rights."

Sitting Wind agreed with him. Perhaps, by fighting alongside other Canadians, they would be able to achieve better recognition for Stoneys, in Ottawa. Perhaps they could even succeed in securing a voice in Parliament to represent Stoney concerns.

He visited Grandma, a couple of weeks after enlisting, and explained everything to her — what the Germans were plotting, and that he found a sense of purpose in fighting. But he didn't mention the promise of land for veterans.

"Some Germans have already landed by rafts on Canada's east coast, and they are killing people along the shores," he said to Grandma. It was a rumour he had heard.

Grandma remained quiet, studying the bare sun-yellowed hills of McDougall's pastures spread out along the north side of the Bow River. She offered no other comment.

He knows that elders don't approve of their having joined the army. "Them young guys doin' crazy things," they tell each other. They fail to comprehend the reversal of government attitudes, whereby their people are now urged to kill their enemies. "Be careful," they warn one another. "It is a trick to make us go against our Treaty; if we do what they suggest, then they may accuse us of breaking our Peace Treaty. Then they will use it someday as an excuse to take away the Treaty, and eventually our reserve lands."

"McDougall said that from now on a rifle was supposed to be used only to kill animals for our food,'' Grandma once scolded impatiently. ''Not people.'' She considers the old missionary the third most powerful being, next to God and Jesus Christ.

''Things will go bad for us if we don't stick to what he taught and to what we promised,'' she admonished. ''As there are many different Indian tribes who were forbidden to fight one another, so also are there different countries of whitemen who should not fight. We listened to the government when they told us to stop fighting our brothers; so now they should listen to themselves too.'' Her arguments were direct, simple.

Sitting Wind bounces around the bag like a pogo stick, hooking lefts and rights which land in thuds, and throw pockets into the canvas. He doesn't feel satisfied with having other people die to protect the land. He wants to contribute. Demonstrate that he can take charge, that he is committed to his people, that he is a leader. Make the purpose tangible.

''Two minutes, Franky boy! Take it easy, now. Take it easy! Don't wear yourself out on the bag, for God's sake!'' Bruno is swinging towels over his shoulder and dips his hand into a bucket of water to test its temperature.

One thing is certain to Sitting Wind. When it comes to being nervous or scared, all humans are practically the same. They're all scared. No matter what race or culture.

His attitude to whitemen has reversed in that regard. He feels nothing like the way he did before being in the army. Then he had a ridiculous awe, a reverence, almost a fear of white people. The army has opened his eyes. White people become dirty in the same way Indians do; they talk about hookers, drinking, and all those things. And they become tired in the same way Indians do, too: there's no difference. Maybe he used to be scared to fight white people: his fears were a mental block which ended up reinforcing themselves. But he's not scared of them now. He's scared of nothing.

He recalls an assembly at Camrose, about two months after enlistment, when they started training there. There were several thousand recruits gathered in a drill hall for a special visit from an overseas battalion commander.

''The army doesn't need cowards,'' the commander bellowed sternly, galvanized walls and steel pipe rafters clanging echos. ''The army has no use for them. Only the brave will win the war. Cowards work against us, they drag the brave into the mire of despair.''

At that very moment he zeroed in on Joe and Sitting Wind who were standing in the front row, hard boots on concrete and chins up at attention. He hesitated, eyes suddenly warming to a new thought, a terse smile playing in a corner of his mouth.

When he spoke again, his tone was more subdued. "It has become evident to me that Indians are especially brave as volunteers. Like these fellows here, for example," he said pointing to them. "Some of you may think Indians are scum. You may consider them beggars, or drunks in the street. But look at these two men! They are not cowards! I'm told that they were among our first volunteers. Men such as these have learned from the earliest age that only cowards turn their backs on their enemies: that only cowards trade purpose and risk for aimless comfort."

A flurry of shouting and applause penetrates from beyond the training room wall. His opponent must be entering the ring.

"Okay, that's it. We're on," Bruno says. "Let's give it to him, fella."

Sitting Wind can smile nervous encouragement only with his eyes; his mouth is caged. Boxing really is a lonely, silent sport.

It was at Camrose that he met Corporal Ron Wally, a Golden Glove champion. One day he suddenly laid his hand on Sitting Wind's shoulder.

"You show good form," he said. "Maybe you should consider training for the Canadian Boxing championship."

"Sure," Sitting Wind responded without a flinch of hesitation. If a whiteman believed he was good, he was more than ready to believe it himself.

"That's the spirit. I think you can do it."

Wally started training him, every evening, with unrelenting confidence in Sitting Wind's ability.

When he was transferred to Currie Barracks the major in charge immediately inquired about his boxing. He said he had received a letter from Camrose.

"Private Kaquitts, are you interested in this next bout?" He eyed Sitting Wind's small stature dubiously.

"Yes."

"All right. You seem rather small but this letter recommends you, so I'll see you through. Just remember one thing," he added paternally. "If, at any point, you feel you cannot continue, inform me so I can get you out."

Sitting Wind emerges from his dressing room, Bruno in the lead. This is it: the evening's main attraction. He sports yellow gloves, the best available, and white army trunks with red and blue stripes down the leg. He's becoming accustomed to a jaw-guard.

He has fought thirty-four bouts so far, with no losses. The training has made his body strong and muscular. He now weighs one hundred and sixty-five pounds, and his clothes have become confining around his wrists, his neck, his chest.

The drill hall is full, the ring surrounded with bleachers submerged under a babbling of personnel and soldiers from the base, as well as members of the public from Calgary. All are here for an evening of entertainment. People are standing in short passageways between the bleachers, eyes craning over heads and berets. Joe is somewhere among them, but Sitting Wind does not try to locate him now.

People's eyes are on him, evaluating him. He hears their voices, "It's an Indian! Wonder what he can do." A glance into the ring confirms that his opponent is already there, rolling his muscles and worrying the crowd into a state of expectation.

Edging along behind Bruno, Sitting Wind is suddenly stricken with awe at Curly's size; not so much the height as the powerful chest development. He's more massive than any opponent he has ever had to face and more forbidding, greased leg and arm muscles bulging, maroon gloves dangling alongside red blue striped shorts.

Adrenalin tremors rushing through his chest cause Sitting Wind to suck in air involuntarily. "This could be it, the end of my line," he thinks. The air is thick with sound and sweat and smoke. He must beat this man, this superman of the ring.

After clambering up the steps and into the circle, Bruno raises Sitting Wind's arm. A microphone screeches.

"And the challenger, ladies and gentlemen, weighing in at one hundred and sixty-five pounds is Frank Kaquitts, a Stoney Indian born and raised at Morley, Alberta."

Sitting Wind casts his eyes defiantly around the crowd; no matter what the odds, he's in it now, and he will be a tough undaunted Indian, never beaten without a hell of a fight.

Bruno pulls him into the corner briefly, furrows between his eyebrows. "He looks pretty easy, Franky boy," he reassures him, a hand on Sitting Wind's shoulder. "You can peg him good."

The bell rings and a referee is ready in the center. Curly is fast, intimidating. Sitting Wind jockeys for position in circles, skirting the ropes, defensive, feeling out his opponent's ways of leading and pulling. He also watches for opportunities, small holes through which he might possibly jab away some of the confidence with which the giant taunts him.

Curly's punches are lightning, and several barge through Sitting Wind's gloved defense, landing squarely on his chest, stunning his eardrums. Shouts from beyond the ropes are like animal sounds. "Give the Indian a chance! Make him fight!" Sitting Wind's confidence shakes, the very platform feeling unstable, unpredictable. He is going to get cleaned. Never in his life has he felt a more desperate need for help.

"Give me my song today, Great Wind Spirit!" he pleads in silence, frantic. "My song! My song! I need my song!" But no one listens. No voice answers from within.

The winner will fight a national champion. What does it matter?

Anger and frustration mounting, Sitting Wind becomes careless and aggressive, flailing, attacking Curly directly with a volley of wild jabs and arcs. For a brief moment his opponent is taken aback, relinquishes ground. But Curly comes right back, entering below a long desperate reach of Sitting Wind's, and wings a right hook solidly into Sitting Wind's ear.

Sitting Wind reels, nerves instantly freezing up. "Don't fall! Whatever you do, don't fall!" All past commands and careful instructions whirl like snowflakes in his head. The bleachers are winding in tight circles. A split second later, after concentrating intently, Sitting Wind again feels his fingers inside the gloves, bends them, feels his arms, his neck. He blinks his blurred eyes. And his eyes, focussed now and sharp, find Curly again. He dances around Sitting Wind like a bear, cautious, but searching for a clean swipe that will end the match.

Sitting Wind engages himself again, angered now that his opponent has made it appear an easy victory. The commander's words come back to him: "These here Indians are bravest of all." And he is Sitting Wind, who is supposed to have a song to call upon the Wind. If only the song would come to him! Come to him now! Why does the Spirit not help? Not answer?

No, he will not hand over defeat in the first round of ten. Even without his song he will prove a bitter opponent. He is a Stoney, fighting for all his brothers, all his family. He is fighting for Treaty rights, for purpose, and for future. Like Sitting Bull, he will never hand over defeat. Will never give up! Will never allow his people to be disgraced.

They dance and circle, eying one another. The bell signals, and they drop into their corners.

Early in the second round Sitting Wind jabs Curly unexpectedly on the nose, blood spraying out the way it blows from nostrils of a deer before it dies. The crowd is astonished. He hears voices, exclamations, which revive his adrenalin and confidence.

He aims again, his yellow gloves sprayed with warm blood. He hears Joe and his other buddies shouting close at hand: ''Hit him again! Hit him again, Franky!'' they call.

Another jab, on an eye this time, plasters blood over Curly's vision and forces him to make spasmodic wiping motions with his gloves to keep his eyes clear. Sitting Wind works with his opponent's indecision, jabbing straight to his nose every time he wipes his eyes, and jabbing his eyes whenever he moves to protect his nose.

The audience's mood is shifting dramatically. Sitting Wind feels his anger and gritty determination dominated by a new and bolder possibility: perhaps he can force an even match here, a very respectable fight of which the Stoneys can be proud. He circles around Curly with increased energy, interspersing his bloody jabs with several left hooks into Curly's solar plexus — weakening the superman, searching for openings to deliver more devastating blows. If he can maintain this pace, could he win this fight? Could he bring him slowly down?

The bell rings again and they retreat to their corner stools. Sitting Wind glances toward his opponent: blood is being wiped from his eyes and face. Bruno is jabbering beside Sitting Wind, excited beyond control.

''Ye got 'im on the rocks, Franky boy! I canna believe what I'm seein' you do, lad! Ye got 'im on the rocks! Just 'it 'im on the chin now, lad, and you'll put 'im right down. Remember the chin swing. You'll get 'im for sure.''

Sitting Wind briefly goes over instructions in his mind: straight out, and then a slightly downward arc upon contact.

In the third round the boxers circle one another more cautiously, like elk with antlers locked. Sitting Wind initiates aggressive jabs designed to draw Curly out. His opponent takes the bait and Sitting Wind immediately finds his chance, hitting him on the nose again, reviving the flow of blood. A fresh blow on Curly's eye smears his vision once more, and Curly's gloves hinge up, instinctively now, to protect this most vulnerable area. Sitting Wind squares him solidly on the chin.

Knockouts are ungracious: a tongue coming loose, joints suddenly limp, eyes momentarily glazed like a dead man's.

''You got him! Hit him again!'' he hears a soldier shouting louder than the others beside the ring. The muscles crumble, staggering. Sitting Wind hooks a right to Curly's ear, and another with a left. Three times in machine-gun succession; his own arms tired, leaden. The superman collapses to the floor like flabby meat on bones.

All around the ring there is shouting, screaming: victory!

The referee holds up Sitting Wind's arm, and parades him around the ring, Bruno in tow — clasping a towel and frantically attempting to share the recognition.

"We love the Indian," he hears the crowd cheering. "We love the Furious Indian! We love Furious Frank!"

"Furious Frank!" A chorus begins to emerge from the crowd. Over and over again they shout, "Furious Frank! Furious Frank!"

For several moments, Sitting Wind allows himself to believe in his victory. But almost as quickly, his smile fades.

The song was not returned to him. The victory is incomplete. The realization arouses a new surge of frustration; frustration more extreme in its dimensions than any aroused by his opponent's punches.

Jerking his wrist free from the referee's moist grip, Sitting Wind lunges at the ropes.

"Furious Frank! Furious Frank!" the crowd clamours, without letting up.

"Ganutha Inghay!" He finds himself shouting the Stoney words, venomously, in return, violently shaking the ropes. "I am Ganutha Inghay!" I am Sitting Wind: the words seem to have been thrust, involuntarily, from deep within him.

But the crowd responds with still louder applause, encouraging what they perceive as an outburst of victory-emotion. "Furious Frank! Furious Frank!"

"No! I am Ganutha Inghay!" He shakes the ropes again. But the crowd drowns his desperate words.

"C'mon! C'mon! Let's get to the showers, Frank," Bruno says, tugging his arm impatiently, and waving to the fans.

Calgary Train Station
September, 1944

"I better be boarding now!" Joe Poucette shouts at the several Stoneys who are sending him off.

Despite the volume he's added to his voice, it barely rises above the blasts and hisses of locomotive pressure valves. Gusts of wind push swirls of cold air and paper litter along the concrete platform. He has extended his hand for final goodbyes; his pose includes a satisfied grin. One by one his relatives respond with a traditional handshake, adding a couple of words to wish him well.

In tandem with their training program, Joe's enthusiasm has been building for months, and is now approaching a climax. The war is on. The action commences. Joe is proud that his friends and family have come to see him off.

A melee of faces criss-crosses before and behind them, the people wearing expressions of urgency, strange mixtures of elation and anxiety.

"All aboard! All aboard!" bellows a platform conductor. Mothers dab their eyes with handkerchiefs.

As Joe turns, Sitting Wind grabs his uniform sleeve. "Wait! I'd like to shake your hand once more."

Joe faces his barracks partner, offering his hand firmly.

"I know you're not actually my brother." Sitting Wind speaks seriously. "But, in a way, you are my brother. I feel as if we're brothers, after all we've been through this past year." The words are partially carried away by wind and commotion.

With his left hand pinning down his beret to prevent its being swept by wind from his neatly combed head, Joe's eyes briefly find those of Sitting Wind, and indicate that his feelings are the same. But now is not the time to be sentimental. His mind is already in England, Europe, Germany, or wherever it is they will be sent. His body must simply follow.

"I'll write you letters, buddy!" he promises. He turns and enters a coach, as a flute-like locomotive whistle signals their start.

"By the way! I'm sorry!" Sitting Wind shouts after him. "About not being able to join you!"

But if Joe has heard, he gives no indication. Briefly, framed by the coach portal at the top of steps, he turns to wave. Steel couplings clang in a thundering rumble down the train's entire length, and the line begins to inch forward.

Unsettled that Joe has not heard him, Sitting Wind attempts a hobbling dash toward the slowly departing coach portal, in order to repeat his apology. But his crutches do not mesh with the shoes and legs of other well-wishers crowded at the platform's edge, waving hats and hands at coach windows. Joe's back has disappeared into the train, and Sitting Wind cannot find his friend's face in any of the windows. How he wanted to be with him on this train. To continue together. If not for the war that the elders argue against, then at least for the adventure.

"I wanted to be sure he understands that I'm sorry," Sitting Wind repeats apologetically to Joe's brother, Felix. Sitting Wind's breathing is laboured, gasping. The noise of spouting steam, steel wheels, and people shouting is too great to permit much conversation.

The Stoney group watches silently, clustered together, until the last of the grinning faces under berets have rolled by and the terminal coach begins to shrink toward a distant apex of parallel steel. Sitting Wind draws a small comfort from the fact that, in the other direction, these tracks still connect Joe to the Morley reserve.

"I guess you feel bad that your foot got gashed, eh?" Felix breaks the ponderous silence settling among them.

Sitting Wind studies Felix's expression for any hint of cynicism. Some people have suggested that it was not an accident; that he deliberately cut his own foot with his grandma's axe so that he would not have to serve overseas. But it is a wicked lie.

"I feel bad," Sitting Wind replies. "Because I didn't want him to go alone. I feel as if he's my brother, too."

"Maybe he should have stayed here also," Felix says wistfully. "Maybe it was a sign."

Sitting Wind considers the content of Felix's words. "A sign? I don't understand. How would there be a sign?"

"Elders say that your accident is a message. A warning that the fighting is not right. They believe that Joe should have stayed here, too.

Sitting Wind attempts no response. Perhaps it is fruitless to believe in old Spirits. Perhaps the missionaries were right all along.

Morley
May, 1950

Kathleen is the prettiest girl on the reserve. That explains why Sitting Wind is on his way to see her again. He has been going more often, lately.

Trigger, his horse, is swaying beneath him in the crisp morning hour, her ears alert, swivelling this way and that as she walks, savouring the sounds of the wilderness and identifying its activity. Moist heat from her back is pushing through the saddle-blanket, warming Sitting Wind's buttocks and the insides of his legs.

It is mid-morning and the sun has risen well above the eastern ridge; it glares into his eyes. He should maybe have waited until later in the day when the sun will be higher. But considering the two-and-a-half to three hour trip from his camp at Rabbit Lake to Kathleen's place at Morley, additional delay would mean arriving back rather late. Besides, today a special dinner is planned for him.

The air is clean, like cool water on his face and in his nostrils. The meadows are alive with the trill and flutter of spring's newly arrived residents. A pair of brilliantly coloured bluebirds yo-yo across the pasture and land on separate fence-posts adjacent to an aspen. Rebirth breathes all around, the upper meadows mixed with stands of freshly greening trees, and the mountains looming sharply in the west against cerulean sky.

Trigger's steps gain a crest of ridge overlooking the Bow River valley and they begin their gradual descent, the two of them absorbed by a vast hill-scape. Sitting Wind studies the ribbon of water snaking in from the west through an uneven gorge cut into the flats. It widens and straightens near Morley where it melds with the Ghost Reservoir, a short distance ahead of the steel bridge at the residential school. Because run-off has begun, the water is greener and brighter than usual.

But the school buildings next to the river appear older and dustier now than they used to be, their crisp white walls faded to greys. Ever since Mr. Staley left, it seems, they have not been kept up as well.

Sitting Wind is twenty-five years old now. Not a youngster any more. It was some twelve years ago that he was last in school; a long time in the past, and so much has happened in the meantime.

When the war and his army days ended, he faded for a while, too. His enthusiasm for the future fell into a sleep, a listless hibernation far away from whitemen, from fighting, from adventure in distant lands. Not that he'd failed in any way. On the contrary, he was a winner, boxing his way to the top: an outstanding athlete. And he'd received two medals on short ribbons to pin to the breast of his uniform. His was an example of achievement for fellow Indians to be proud of.

But other things became oppressive afterward: the accidental gashing of his foot with Grandma's axe, which prevented him from serving overseas; the hollow offer of veterans' land which, if he'd accepted, would have required living far removed from his family and friends on the reserve, and having to pay back debts.

"You sign this paper and we'll find you a farm, and include all the necessary equipment," the discharge officer said decisively, eyeing him. "You'll have eighteen years to repay it, and the government will not tax you during that time. You couldn't ask for a better deal. All you have to do is move onto the farm and you're the owner."

Sitting Wind thought about it. If he had to pay it back he would probably go broke because he doesn't know enough about farming any more to handle it successfully.

"I don't think I'll be able to do that," he'd responded. But, he thinks in retrospect, perhaps he should have accepted, and hired someone to manage it for him.

"Suit yourself," the officer replied. "Of course, another option is to take $44,000. You can do with it as you please, but you must pay it back over 18 years."

But how would he ever pay it back? They would probably throw him in jail should he fail.

He left him there holding the papers.

Joe never made it back. That's what really shook him. He received letters from him for a while, but a German's bullet suddenly silenced him, alone in a strange country. The letters stopped, unfinished. He never came back.

Kathleen lives well past the Trading Post, at the far end of Chiniki Village flat, not too distant from Grandma's old cabin. She has been trying to attract his interest since last year, or maybe even earlier. But he was not ready, and he pretended a lack of interest so that she would not form ideas too soon about settling down or becoming dependant on him. He was not ready for anything serious.

The hunting and trapping life offers the benefit of being able to withdraw from the mainstream of hope and excitement without having to say to people like Mr. Rodgers, "I'm not doing much of anything, really. Just bumming around." But it is not that remarkable either, the hunting and the trapping. Uncle Josiah taught him well, and there is a peace to be found in wilderness: a soothing knowledge that survival is at least always possible, if not always desirable. The pace is so much more relaxed, only the simple expectations of your body requiring its food and warmth. Even girls he could do without. They had ways of imposing their own expectations.

Recently, however, he has started feeling more enthusiastic about the relationship, his eyes regaining some of their boyhood brightness, becoming clearer like today's sky. Lately, he has noticed, his thoughts are including her more and more in plans. She seems to have a good effect on him: there is no doubt about that in his mind, and he rather likes it.

"I have noticed that you like Kathleen. You have been seeing her every once in a while since last year," her father said to him last week. "I have asked her mother to make a special dinner for you. We want you to come." He felt the skin in his neck tighten, tingle. It was a special invitation.

He and Trigger climb up the other side of the valley, and as they skirt the flank of a ridge, the Trading Post slides into view. It is nudged like a barely-rooted cactus, against the straight steel of railroad tracks stretching from the eastern horizon to the west. The siding is weathered grey, scoured by tiny airborne grains of silt picked up by gusty Chinooks or sucked up by horse hooves passing, blasting every vertical construction in their horizontal drift. Even the three scrawny contorted aspens near the front owe their survival to a scant protection of store front. The windows are small dusty port-holes and he can see no horses at the railing.

The pow wow at Easter time is still fresh in his mind. It was at the Chiniki Village Community Hall, a six-sided log roundhouse with a dirt floor, and the drummers all huddled in the center. Kathleen was standing against the west wall among other women, with her mother. She was laughing and talking with other girls, hiding her face in her hands from time to time. The older women, bright kerchiefs over their braids, squatted on their blankets.

He was with the men on the other side, the east side. There were white visitors too, seated on a small bench set up against a wall opposite the entrance: special government guests connected with the Trans-Canada Highway which they are planning to build through the reserve.

Sitting Wind enjoys pow-wows and looks forward to them eagerly. He is one of the best chicken dancers and was made champion at Banff Indian Days last summer.

According to Stoney custom any male who wishes to dance with a girl must go and stand by the drummers, his back turned to the females, and wait for a girl to select him. The girls watch to see which boys are making their way to the center. Kathleen must have been watching for him to make his move, because she was right there as soon as he melded into the circle of booming rhythm, her slight finger poking gently into the small of his back. He turned his head, saw her eyes: oblique, questioning. She was even shorter than he, it struck him again; exactly the right height for him.

Mr. Rodgers is behind his counter. The store smells of harness and smoked skins.

"How are you doin', Frank? Come out to visit Kathleen again?" Mr. Rodgers laughs. He is always cheerful. He likes the Stoney people.

"I guess you could say so," Sitting Wind says. "I need a couple of things at the store anyway. Thought I might as well come out for a ride."

"You know, you ought to forget Rabbit Lake and move in a little closer. The hell, seems to me you're spendin' most of your time here anyhow. Why don't you marry the girl and have it over with, eh? Settle down and raise a family?"

Mr. Rodgers has a way of being tuned in to people's thoughts. He knows just where things are at without asking too many questions.

Sitting Wind ponders this for a moment, digging money for snuff from his pocket. He's met girls before. But they were not the same.

"Look. There's my father in the tepee village," she said to him, daring to point with only a slight motion of her finger while her hands clutched the safety bar enclosing their descending ferris wheel seat. "Maybe he's searching for me. He doesn't know where I went."

The thickly-peopled Stampede Grounds were spread out beneath them like a large canvas crawling with tiny berries, red ones, blue, green, yellow, and orange. He explored her face then, her brown eyes drawing out his strength: his will to succeed, to climb to the top. How could he resist those eyes? His arms were around her, he was kissing her as they fell through sky.

He'd marry her any day. But right now? He would have to look after her; there would probably be kids. Where would he work? There are hardly any jobs around. Marriage still seems remote.

"I'm invited to a special dinner at Johnny Chiniquay's place tomorrow," he informed Grandma as she emerged from behind a clump of spruce. She was limping more than she used to, holding a hide scraper in her hand like an arthritic bone. So aged, she appears lately. But she smiled mischievously, as if she knew more than he did himself. "It would be good manners to clean yourself before you go. And wear your good jacket."

Sitting Wind scans a shelf behind Mr. Rodgers with unfocussed eyes. "One of these days I suppose I should settle down, stop running around. But I'll need to work and make some money. Which reminds me of something I wish to ask you: do you ever need a helper in your store, now and then?"

"I'm afraid I can't oblige you, Frank. There's simply not enough work here for anyone but me and my wife."

"That's okay."

"You should talk to the CPR section boss. He sometimes needs a new man, especially with the summer coming on."

This sounds like a good prospect. Mr. Rodgers offers to check into it on his behalf, provided Sitting Wind promises not to tell other Stoneys. He does not want a lineup arriving in pursuit of similar favours.

"I'll be seeing you later," Sitting Wind calls over his shoulder halfway through the exit as he leaves. The horse sniggers in greeting, her ears trained with interest on a cluster of mares across the tracks westward. He brings her head about and directs her into the last stretch, toward the bottom of Scott Lake hill.

The new highway is going to pass right through there, which is why the government will build a new place for John Chiniquay soon. This old one is not much bigger than Grandma's cabin; but it is better kept.

Kathleen approaches the table carrying a bowl steaming with the aroma of saskatoons. The berries were preserved by drying last fall, and now they've been cooked in sugar. In silence she passes the bowl from one person to the next, each taking a ladleful onto his plate. The main course of beef stew was steeped in smooth gravy, and mixed with lush potato chunks. A hearty and delicious meal. But this dessert is a still more special treat. Sitting Wind cannot help smiling as the purple berries flow into his plate.

There are more people here than he expected; not only her parents but also Kathleen's uncle, and elder Paul Mark and his wife. Maybe they are friends of her parents. Or, Sitting Wind wonders, could they have been invited for some special purpose?

"Let the great Creator be good to us old people so that we can live happy lives in our old age, and also to young people when they are just beginning as families, starting out on their own," Paul Mark prayed at the meal's beginning.

They eat in silence. Heavy log walls hold them together as a group, but each person's thoughts remain individual, private. Trigger's flank is visible across the table through small squares of glass in the window, tail hanging relaxed. The nice thing about spring is that there are no flies yet to bother horses. Sitting Wind feels the berries smooth and tangy in his mouth; when they are hot they taste sharper. A vague memory of camps at James River sifts through his mind.

He is conscious of having no rights here: he cannot just say anything which comes to mind. The elders are to be respected.

Paul Mark places his spoon on his empty plate and raises his eyes to Kathleen's father. "Better this way than if we eat them from the bush," he beams.

Kathleen's father laughs with him. "Maybe you like them more sweet like this with sugar added, eh." He is licking the purple sauce along his bottom lip. The others laugh too, Kathleen smiling shyly into her plate.

"Now that we have eaten this good food I desire to raise a matter for discussion." Kathleen's father is suddenly serious, after a thoughtful pause and glance at Sitting Wind. "It is about couples who are interested in each other and should consider starting their lives together."

Sitting Wind glances at Kathleen, whose eyes are riveted to the bottom of her plate, where she is re-routing small rivulets of sauce. He allows his eyes briefly to meet those of her father, acknowledging that he is listening respectfully.

"It is not an easy thing for a man to decide on taking a woman for his wife, and to make a living for her and her children. That is why I have asked elder Paul Mark to eat with us, so he can explain what is involved."

He wants us to get married, Sitting Wind suddenly realizes with shock. He is unprepared for this moment. Kathleen is licking her spoon. He reviews his thoughts once more, racing them through his mind too fast to allow his voice to engage with any that make sense, with any that would sound grown-up.

"My wife and myself, we have noticed you take an interest in our daughter Kathleen and visit with her, and she also has told us that she wishes to live with you like husband and wife." The formality of the opening sentences weigh heavily on Sitting Wind, laden as they are with the gravity of responsibilities. "We have thought about this matter and talked it over with your grandma and with Josiah. They agreed that you would make a successful couple and have told us to go ahead and bring this up with you, persuade you to start this new way of living."

Sitting Wind studies the scars of his hand, propped up on his chest in a crook of his other arm. There must be a reason for waiting. "Why don't you marry the girl and have it over with," Mr. Rodgers said. But maybe he should wait for another half year because he will be busy travelling around for rodeos. Kathleen may not much enjoy the travelling around. She would be better off with her parents.

On the other hand it would make their meetings much more relaxed. Her mother always watches her closely, especially when he comes to see her. He is permitted only to talk with her indoors, and her family observes him to see what kind of a person he is.

Elder Mark smiles evenly, in a fatherly way at them. He has been married for a long time, and is wise in how people should treat one another and live with one another.

"I know the reserve is changing, and our way of living is changing too." He clears his throat in preparation for what is to follow. Kathleen's father settles back in his chair, rolling tobacco for a cigarette, making ready to listen. "But when it comes to living as a husband and wife, these things don't change much. So listen closely to what I am going to say to you. I will give you advice which will be of help.

"In the early days young people had to earn their marriages because they would be facing hardships ahead of them. They would have to be prepared to challenge all hardships together, without help from their parents. That is why we Stoneys believe it is not healthy for a person to get married at an early age; the boys should first be trained in hunting and handling horses. A person has to be qualified to keep a wife.

"Similarly a girl is not ready to be married until she knows how to handle all kinds of hides of buffalo, moose, deer, and all kinds of fur bearing animals. In this way she will be a help to her husband when they are alone some place away out in wild country.

"However, when a young woman and a young man are ready, as I think you are, and if they are interested in each other, then they should make their life together. That's the way it has always been."

In a silence which follows, Sitting Wind looks up at elder Mark, and notes with relief that he appears to have ended already. Is he worried they are not old enough? They are all waiting for some response.

"I think I would like to be married with Kathleen," he begins supportively. "We have been seeing each other for quite a while now, and I learned how to survive with hunting and trapping as it was taught to me by my uncle, Josiah. But I have a feeling that right now may not be the best time."

A quick glance in Kathleen's direction reveals no reaction yet to his carefully selected words. "The reason being that I'm a cowboy," he hears himself continuing. "Which means I'll be on the road a lot during the summer, moving from rodeo, to rodeo, sort of thing. I kinda doubt she would much enjoy that."

"It does not matter what you will be doing," elder Mark cuts in heavily. "You can take her along as your wife, as long as you look after her well and don't leave her stranded somewhere on her own. When you take her, you have to stop fooling around with your friends, drinking, the things that young people do before they settle down."

Sitting Wind tries to push his chair back from the table, but the wall is immediately behind him, cramping his quarters. There are no arguments strong enough here. He glances at Kathleen who is still studying her plate. She appears to be waiting for some resolution.

"Maybe you should ask Kathleen, to see whether she would like to accompany you to rodeos," suggests her father.

Sitting Wind waits for her eyes to ascend briefly to his own. But they betray nothing. If anything, they are vacant, afraid of opinion, afraid to assert their craving for him as her husband, lest she should be rejected.

"Would you go with him to rodeos, if he wants you to go?" her father asks her directly. There is a hint of impatience in his voice.

She nods.

Sitting Wind catches her slight nod. There is no way out.

Right now is a good time as any then, he thinks: I've got to do it sometime, regardless.

Elder Paul Mark is suddenly shaking his hand, and his wife following, and then his new father- and mother-in-law, and Kathleen's uncle. They are happy. Kathleen is happy too.

He is happy.

It seems Grandma does not expect him back tonight because she knew about the dinner, and about the plans.

"You may as well stay here for tonight," Kathleen's mother tells him. "The bed is big enough for both of you."

Hobbema
February, 1953

Snow is falling. The flakes are not as large or wet as they are in March; they are small, densely crowded in the bitter cold. The hood and windshield of Sitting Wind's car slowly wedge themselves through a thick grey curtain as he motors along well rutted drifts toward the Hobbema community church. Josiah is beside him, and his Cree brother Ed. In the rear seat are Ed's wife and four children. She is impatiently admonishing them to quit horsing around.

"A fella can get lost in zis weather," Josiah mutters in his deeply accented English.

Sitting Wind does not respond. His intense concentration is on the cloud of snow he is following, an occasional glimpse of chrome bumper or black fender emerging through swirls. It's a grim day for those people whose only transport is a horse and sled, he considers. Now that he has his own car he can go pretty well anywhere.

Josiah leans over and drools expertly into a pop bottle tucked between his legs. Because Moraha lived with him and his father Ben for so many years at Morley and at Rabbit Lake, Josiah no longer considered her as merely his father's Cree wife. She was his mother, as good as any mother could be, and she appeared perfectly at home with Stoney people at Morley. And Frank: he is like a young brother. Yes, his young brother.

With his left glove Sitting Wind tries to erase further condensation freezing to the inside of his windshield.

"My time is coming," she said reflectively one evening, a couple of months ago. Josiah was seated with them. "I wish to return to Hobbema and spend my last days with my true families around. I wish you to take me there, tomorrow."

Sitting Wind had purchased a car only recently, and she'd sat quietly, bracing the dashboard with her crooked hand. She'd asked if he was travelling too fast.

Paul, another of Sitting Wind's Cree brothers, left the house an hour ago on horse and sled, Grandma lying frozen in the back. She'd told them that she wished the ceremony to be conducted the old way, the way of her fathers and grandfathers: not in a hearse, or with any fancy coffin purchased from a store.

The car lurches in a veering motion as the right wheel is sucked into loose snow. Sitting Wind swings sharply left, struggling to regain a safe course. The fan motor is droning: blasts of semi-warm air maintain small, frost-free ovals on the glass.

"How come Gramma has to die?" he hears one of the children whimper in the rear.

He finds it difficult to follow conversations in Cree now. Throughout his life he has become used to Stoney language.

"Hush, you silly child!" its mother reprimands in an impatient tone. "Don't you know anything? Everybody has to die sometime." She pauses: suddenly hearing the words that came from her mouth. Then, as if trying to undo their harsh irreverence, she adds a brief smile to the rear-view mirror. "When a person is good then she may at least live to an old age."

"Good thing you didn't bring your wife and your kid, that's for sure," Ed interrupts, to Sitting Wind.

Sitting Wind eases on the accelerator as a vehicle ahead has slowed, and the blizzard in its wake is settling. Kathleen cried softly, privately when their first baby Doreen died. An infant, one month old; it was not very long after they started living together. The coffin was small, not much larger than one of those orange crates discarded behind the Trading Post. Kathleen dressed her in pink, because Mrs. Rodgers advised her that girl babies wear pink.

"She wanted to come, but you know how it is with babies. Anything can happen in weather like this. Kind of dangerous. She thought it might be better to stay behind with the others."

The others are Kathleen's parents, in their new cabin which has rooms, and smooth wood floors, a large stove, and stucco on the outside plastered with pop-bottle gravel which glitters in morning sun.

After the surprise dinner which Kathleen's mother prepared, he remained with his new wife's family for two weeks in their cabin. Then he took her to Rabbit Lake where they settled down in a tepee next to Josiah's family and Grandma. Grandma showed Kathleen how she cured hides and prepared food; but Moraha was becoming old and crippled. That first winter was cold and long, hunting and trapping with Josiah. Many meals were nothing more than rabbit stew.

Gerald was born the following year, in their tent next to the railroad tracks at Morley. After Sitting Wind started with the CPR Kathleen and Grandma became good friends.

"She doesn't really know anyone here anyways," Sitting Wind adds as an afterthought. "And she could be a little shy about it."

He was lucky to obtain that CPR job. Mr. Rodgers helped him, assured the whiteman that Sitting Wind was a good worker. In preparation for winter his crew tightens bolts, straightens rails. If a rail snaps during cold weather they replace it with a new one, working quickly between the comings and goings of trains under long plumes of black smoke.

Some workers complain about small wages, but he is satisfied, excited in fact about a steady job which gives him money every two weeks for groceries and supplies. A week after starting he moved their tepee from Rabbit Lake and pitched it up behind the Trading Post, within a stone's throw of the track. He would be right there, ready in case of any trouble.

Gerald was born a couple of years ago last fall, barely a year after the first baby died, as the season's first Chinook winds whipped the canvas violently. He should have camped on the other side of that hill, where it was less open to the flats.

The snowfall has eased off substantially as they draw up to the church. His eyes center on Paul's sled, with a Union Jack draped over the side, snugged against the church steps. It is difficult to identify heavily bundled Crees located on and behind it, pulling Grandma in her coffin off the wooden platform and up the stairs. He is almost late; they could have waited for him to help.

Assorted other sleds have been deposited around the church, harnessed horses with heads drooped to fence-posts waiting patiently in brittle air, nostrils steaming. The sleds are simple, homemade; rough cut saw-board platforms and benches bolted to a single set of bobs. Horse ears twist toward them alertly as car doors snap behind them. They meet other late-comers who have approached, a man and wife fixed like wax to a front seat, and grandparents with kids wrapped in short thick coats and bright shawls wedged behind them, in scant shelter from wind. When their horse stops the figures unfold stiffly.

"Hello, Amos," Sitting Wind says with a grave nod. They shake hands, but it is not the right time for additional conversation. The families look each other over, nodding acknowledgments as they converge at the entrance.

The church is plain whitewashed shiplap, and a cone of steps funnelling into its vestibule is scraped of snow, the boards worn smooth from passages of shoes and rubber galoshes. As he enters, a cold blast of air enters around him; the floor is brittle and resonant under his leather boots. The rows of tall trellis windows lining each wall only thinly separate the interior from the colder exterior.

There is beauty in the outdoors behind glass, Sitting Wind reflects. Even now. A wash of grey firmament domes white snow drifts, which shift along grassy flats between spikes of black aspen.

As his eyes adjust to the semi-light, he makes out people on benches, faces he has never smiled with. They are not the same as Stoneys. A wood stove is crackling coldly near the front, and his measured steps take him directly toward the black-draped coffin which has just been brought in and settled on a table before the pulpit. It is simple, as she wished it, made of rough boards by her grandsons. But the black cloth is light, almost silky. She would have relished the feel of it, her thick fingers like sausages sliding on its surface, tasting its delicacy.

"Psst, Frank!" a voice whispers at his left.

It is Paul, signalling him. The bench is cold, unyielding. Josiah and Ed sit down with him, but the women and children split off to the benches on the right side, as is customary.

He can see people seated behind the pulpit now. Some must be singers, musicians. And elders who knew Grandma when she was younger and lived in Hobbema with Sam Cecil. She once told him that she used to travel in a Red River cart, in the old days when she was young. She used to go all the way into Saskatchewan, areas she knew from her own childhood. Crees may have migrated from this direction once, long ago.

Also seated behind the pulpit is Sitting Wind's father, John. He appears different wearing a red checkered wool coat, and underneath it a light shirt and grey silk tie grotesquely adorned with brocaded flowers. His eyes are fixed to the back of the church, as if he could stare straight through the pulpit and over the heads of his much younger wife and their eleven children.

"You should visit your father once in a while in Hobbema," Grandma urged patiently when Sitting Wind was discharged from the army. "He knows you, because you're his son." Sitting Wind had never seen his father; could find no picture of him in his imagination, no sound to describe his voice.

"I don't know him," he replied. "In fact I would feel sorta like a stranger there, even with my own brothers, because I can't speak Cree. We'd have to speak English when we talk."

"He is still your father, and he said he wants to see you," she persisted. "He has not seen you for more than ten years, since you were small and started going to school in Morley. I'll tell your brothers to go with you. Then you will see him."

The brothers had walked boldly into their Hobbema house. Additional relatives were gathered, joking and laughing because Sitting Wind was going to meet his father for the first time, and this was a happy occasion. But speaking English to him and attempting to address him as "Dad" was enormously uncomfortable. How could he call a stranger "Dad"?

Cree people were different from Stoneys in their customs: the relatives all kissed him, even the men. It felt silly to be kissed by another man, right in front of everyone. He thought they must have made a mistake; this could not be his dad.

"You may come and visit any time you wish," his father's other wife assured Sitting Wind. "You could even stay here if you like."

But his father frowned at her for saying that. He saw his father frown, and knew it was because he already had too many kids in the house.

"Dear brothers and sisters." The minister's voice is soothing. "It is in the name of our Lord God, our Heavenly Father, that we have come together today to bring home our beloved Moraha Kaquitts Cecil."

A child from somewhere behind Sitting Wind begins bawling loudly, its wails melding with the tones of the minister's incantations. The minister smiles serenely at the blessed humanity of children crying through his words. The window frames creak and groan and the stove has started warming air in the front rows.

"I wonder what it is like to die," he asked her once.

She gazed through his eyes for a long time before her lips moved again.

"I have been told it will be like a journey," she said, speaking slowly. "There are medicine men who have told stories about it, have heard about it through their Spirit powers. They say that after death there are four levels of existence. Eventually you will achieve the highest level. But not immediately, unless you are a really honest, good person. Very few get to the highest level immediately."

With deep regret, Sitting Wind recalled occasions of drinking too much in downtown bars at night, sneaking into strip shows.

"The lowest level is for murderers. If you end up in the lower level, you will feel all alone. Even though there may be thousands of people with you in the same level — you would never be talking to them.

"If a person steals animals but is not a murderer, he would probably go to the second level. The second level is not as bad. But the third level is still better. And the fourth level is like heaven where you always feel happiness. That is the way you will feel when you are traveling there; that's what it is. You will always feel happiness."

The minister's voice is rising and falling like warm waves breaking on shore.

"... and we all know that Moraha was a good woman, a devoted wife to her first husband Sam Cecil before he was taken away, and thereafter to her second husband Ben Kaquitts of Morley before our Lord called him home. With these thoughts in mind let us sing our favourite hymn, 'In The Sweet Bye And Bye.'"

The singers on stage lead, the minister swinging his arm decisively, encouraging the congregation. Sitting Wind finds his voice, and after several bars it becomes strong, lusty, melding with the melancholy cadence. He misses his grandma now. Her stories, her encouragement, her persistent treatment of him as her child when he had no parents to rely on through all his younger years. Why does even a good person have to die?

He studies her coffin as he sings out, becoming oblivious to the others around him. He imagines her lying within, eyes totally and finally robbed of expression, staring up at the lid, her body stiff and cold, but her heart hearing their beautiful songs and desiring to smile at him warmly, if her dead body would only allow her.

Uncannily, he feels her cold eyes filling his own eye-sockets, her frozen shell of skin encasing him, surrounding him. Is he on his back, staring up with glassy eyes at the darkened grain of pine boards? He wills his arms to move, his hands to push away the closed coffin lids — but they do not obey any more. He wills his lips to part, to sing the song his ears heard as a baby. But his ears are dead. The song is no more.

To counter a sudden stifling anxiety, Sitting Wind forces his attention away from the coffin. The minister's face is washed with kindness and generosity as the congregation repeats the "Sweet bye and bye" refrain with increased vigour and feeling. Perhaps the minister has been right all along, and there is only one God. McDougall's God, who is the same for all people.

"From now on it is up to you and me to make a living together; just you and me," she commented years ago while returning home from Ben's funeral. Her tears had stopped flowing, skin under her eyes still swollen. "He was a good hunter all his life, a good provider," she sighed staring across Morley Flats.

Sitting Wind was only nine years old then: responsibilities loomed enormous. Seated beside her in the bumpy wagon, he followed her eyes over the Flats too, searching; but he could find nothing there.

The minister has now come down to the coffin, opening the

coarsely-crafted lid. In the shuffle of feet Sitting Wind stands up too, joining the relatives to pay their last respects with a kiss on rubber cheeks, or to hold her cold thick hand briefly in passing.

He is comforted that her eyes are closed as if sleeping, a white sheet pulled back below her chin.

She told him to remember his name. His Indian name. "Use it! It will give you power." He regarded her then, through his army eyes, the eyes of a rancher, cowboy. The eyes of a CPR man hammering spikes deep into tar-soaked ties, causing black juice to press from the cracks. What good would the name do nowadays? What place do Indian names have anymore in our way of living?

"Do not think the old ways are not good anymore," she chided gently, as if reading his mind. "Keep respecting our old ways. There will come a time when your eyes will be opened, and the power of your Spirit will be all that you can rely on in your trouble."

"What about becoming a fighter for my people?" he retorted with surprising impatience. "A fighter for Indian rights? A leader? Nothing is happening"

"One day, suddenly, your life will make a turn," she reassured him.

Approaching the casket, Sitting Wind bends his face close to hers, as if to kiss her. There is no aura of warmth. His own breath comes back to him cold, as if bounced from stones. If she is there somewhere it must be only her spirit.

He moves his lips close to her ear and whispers; private words, in Stoney so no one else can hear them. "This is me, Grandma. Sitting Wind. If you can hear me from somewhere in your journey, I'm saying my last goodbye. I guess I'll be on my own now. I may not become anything great. But thanks for looking after me when I was young."

Moraine Lake
August, 1957

Whoever would have speculated that Sitting Wind would become an artist? A Christian artist? Certainly not Grandma. No, certainly not Grandma. Yet, this could be it: this could be the time in his life — which Grandma once predicted — when he would experience a sudden turn of events. It feels right.

He is now in a guitar band too, singing gospel songs on the Reserve; he has also been elected to serve on the Band Council.

Sitting Wind studies the slopes of Mount Babel towering over Moraine Lake. Snows have melted during runoff and, where the deepest drifts were earlier, there are now long runs of pliant willows, their woolly leaves clothed in silver hairs. Avalanches of previous years have cut ascending swaths through spruce and alpine fir, long curved tongues reaching up from soft creek beds where grizzlies dig for wild carrots, to narrow crevices in rocky cliffs. His eyes probe along pockets of small scree, and beyond to strong rock faces; occasionally white goats can be seen crossing, like cartoons on the grey screen of a drive-in theatre.

The mountains have been considered sacred since earliest memories of elders. Probably since the beginning of time or, as the oldest stories claim, since Wesakijack included them in his playground. Sitting Wind recalls warm memories, although they are dim with the passage of time, of riding as a toddler on tepee canvas in back of Grandpa's wagon, returning to Morley after Banff Indian Days: the trail faithfully following the Bow River, Mnee Thnay, panoramas of mountain slopes slowly rocking by. The roads could hardly be considered roads then. Improved wagon trails, perhaps.

Elders have noted that their familiar surroundings are lately changing at an alarming rate. It worries them: the paved roads, the people, the factories, the power dams. But, he is happy here. He is happy with his life. These mountains are like the walls of his home.

Bringing a sliver of charcoal to the canvas before him, Sitting Wind's hand works quickly, decisive strokes committing firm lines to his sketch. The cliffs looming above him consist not of flat slabs like Mount Yamnuska which overlooks the reserve, but of more horizontal lines, blocks of rock like columns which defy erosion instead of stooping with defeated shoulders.

"The Tower of Babel," the nuns called it with a reverence which could equal that applied by ancient Stoneys or cryptic medicine men. Its general appearance is not unlike Castle Mountain where Norman Abraham's father shot a crippled ram before Banff National Park was established, and hunting was prevented.

Whitemen named it from the Holy Bible, Sitting Wind realizes. He does not remember anyone informing him of the mountain's Stoney name. Tower of Babel seems to be a good name. At least it has something to teach people, a lesson from the Holy Book. At the Residential School, Reverend Staley once told them the story of Babel: many people of different languages building a high tower reaching to heaven. Eventually they all spoke the same language. This made God angry, and subsequently the people commenced fighting one another in wars all over the world. If people would listen to the true God, then fighting would never have started, and there would only be love and caring for one another. Sitting Wind believes this. Wars are definitely wrong. He believes firmly now in peace and love for one's fellow man.

In years past he used simply a pencil to make drawings. But Pete Whyte, a famous artist from Banff, showed him charcoal which is better. When you later cover its lines with oils, the pigments will not mix together as pencil lines do, smudging colours.

This morning's light is exceptional. The sun, high before noon, has flooded the valley where most students are scattered, in various working postures, around a gravelly slope at Moraine Lake's north edge. Some, including himself, have clambered to more elevated rock piles to achieve a bird's eye perspective. Two students this year are Catholic nuns: The Two Sisters, other students chuckle. They call to mind a mountain near Canmore, named The Three Sisters. "Ask them what happened to their other sister," they whispered to one another, snickering, in a small group. Even on hot days these gentle women wear long black dresses, silky like the wrap of Grandma's coffin. Of Uncle Josiah's coffin too; he died at the Colonel Belcher Hospital in Calgary, not long after Grandma. They said he drank too much.

One of the teachers he met last year is Reverend Lonsdale of Banff. He is fond of Sitting Wind, and it is his cabin in which he now stays during the week. It is too far to drive every day back and forth to Morley.

This is the second year in succession that he has won a scholarship to the Banff School of Fine Arts, Sitting Wind considers with unabashed satisfaction. It is a hundred dollars, which probably isn't much if you consider the total cost. But Indian Affairs is covering the remainder.

To counter a slight breeze which is nudging at the corner of his sketch pad, threatening to flip a page, Sitting Wind shifts the weight of his left hand. A Clark's nutcracker ratchets raucously from upslope spruce trees. He chuckles to himself when he thinks of how these plump, grey and black lined birds were created by God to make such excessive noise. God must have been in a rambunctious mood that day.

Students are taught to sketch quickly, fifteen of them taken by bus throughout the Bow Valley for the course's initial two weeks. They have visited Johnston Canyon, the Canmore opera hall, and Lake Louise. After the field sketching program ends, they will spend the rest of the summer completing their works indoors.

Sitting Wind prefers oils. They last forever. He wants his new direction in life to last forever.

The CPR job continues to bring steady income during the winter when he is not at art school. The supervisor gave him leave of absence for two months, and he is again welcome back once the course is done. But in all honesty, over the last couple of years, what he once considered as a challenge — to maintain the railway lines — has diminished to drudgery. He knows the job too well now. He is a section man, a boss. There can be no further advancement.

Instead, he has allowed himself to become increasingly convinced that his future lies in art. Isn't it obvious? He wonders that it never dawned on him earlier in life. Every person who views his paintings becomes excited about them. They are selling. Catharine Whyte purchased one for three hundred dollars. Three hundred dollars! And when he finishes his courses he plans to conduct shows like world famous artists do, and sell paintings for great sums of money. God is with him.

"You have a wonderfully strange Indian name," Catharine exclaimed one day while her eyes explored a trail-exhausted pony and rider set sharply against a backdrop of foothills cradling a hunting camp. "I wonder how they conjure up such names?" A pendulum clock in another room of her Banff house chimed lazily.

He studiously avoided answering her question. The name "Sitting Wind" was dormant, if not dead. It belonged to a past life which had little current relevance. It belonged to a different set of beliefs, another religion. To elders and medicine men and strange spiritual tales. It could offer nothing. It was past.

"You should use it as a signature to your paintings," she encouraged. "It is colourful and romantic." But he could muster only a blank smile.

A few threatening clouds have now rolled in, wafting the edges of shadowed cliffs, and breaking up the blanket of sun-spray into beams of light which move over the motley vegetation of lower slopes. Bringing out his palette, Sitting Wind deftly mixes colours and smears small dabs onto the canvas with palette knife, making colour notations. His fingers cool sharply during moments of shade. He compares the results with the real colours contained in the panorama before his eyes. Light conditions are ever fluid, changing.

A manicured middle aged man had opened the door and said,*"Umbah wethstitch,"* a familiar Stoney greeting. "Come on in."

It was Sitting Wind's first introduction to the famed artists, Peter and Catharine Whyte, a couple of years ago, in January. One of Sitting Wind's uncles, George MacLean (more commonly known as Walking Buffalo) had escorted him to their Banff residence. Actually, it was the other way around. He had escorted Walking Buffalo, because his old uncle was unable to drive and had no car of his own. And that's how it had started: Sitting Wind volunteering to be his uncle's chauffeur, and God directing his life to a new road in art.

Peter was delighted to see his frequent visitor, George, and they quickly fell into animated conversation, paying no attention to Sitting Wind. George was quite a talker. Sitting Wind waited patiently. Elders said that Pete and Catharine were interested in the Stoneys, and were always ready to help them by purchasing handicrafts.

Their house felt strange; it was what he might have imagined as the home of a millionaire. It was a log house, filled with artifacts from different countries. The large living room contained tomahawks, peace pipes, bead-work, feather headdresses, and numerous relics displayed on consoles and side-tables. The fireplace was constructed of Rundle rock. There were paintings hanging everywhere on walls. The set of stairs led to an additional room built for their studio — he later found out — featuring small leaded glass windows, similar in size to those in Stoney cabins.

"Would you like coffee or tea?" Catharine finally appeared and interrupted the older men. She was slim, and energetic with a sprightly smile.

"Some tea would be very good! Very good!" George replied,

laughing comfortably at his own dramatics.

Sitting Wind requested the same.

All of a sudden George introduced Sitting Wind.

"Pete, I almost forgot to tell you. This is my nephew, Frank." Again they broke into a fit of laughter, at George's forgetting to introduce his nephew.

"He's a new councillor now and he's a painter too. A good painter. In fact...." He made a serious face and pulled in close to Pete. "He might even be better than you are!" He said this as a joke, and they grinned again.

He was elected councillor only a few weeks earlier: exceptionally young at age thirty-two. Five dollars every meeting, maybe once every month. Johnny Bearspaw was chief.

Pete turned to Sitting Wind, surprised. "So you paint, eh? When you come next time, bring along a few of your paintings. I would like to see your work."

Sitting Wind felt uncomfortably warm then. Suddenly the room was warm.

Almost two years have passed since that day. Now he basks in all the recognition he's getting for his painting, although he is careful not to boast unduly of his ability. There is a sense of well-being to be derived from knowing that one is entrusted by God with a very unique talent.

Gerda Kristofferson was a painter he met twenty years before, and she had encouraged him with some oil paints and brushes. She was camped near Grandma's old cabin, making portraits of John Hunter. She seemed to take a liking to him. It must have been God's plan all along. Sitting Wind was still a young boy in the Residential School then.

Mixing a dab of cerulean blue with green he tests a smear along the toe of slope. It needs a touch more light — he corrects it — to contrast more sharply with the almost fluorescent green water. He is pleased with the final result. Sunshine has again pushed through, but a biting breeze is becoming more contrary, and Sitting Wind is eager to complete his sketch. Perhaps there will be some time remaining to explore the larger rubble, locate features of secret interest: such as grass-drying platforms of tiny rock-rabbits.

Later that memorable day, on the way home from their meeting with Pete and Catharine, his uncle chuckled mischievously. He had money from a sale of moccasins and a beaded vest to Pete. He said to Sitting Wind, "Be sure to bring him a couple of paintings next time you go. You could go next weekend. You may get money for them."

151

It dawned on Sitting Wind that there existed people who made a living from making art. Painting was no different from making handicrafts. It would be easy for him: and fun too.

"I have small ones at home," Sitting Wind assured him. "A tepee under moonlight in the mountains. Another one of horses grazing on the Flats in a Chinook wind."

Sitting Wind's eyes study the water of Moraine Lake. Lakes in the high mountains seem more intensely green than those in the foothills and prairies. "Turquoise", teacher Mr. Phillips described it. Like Navajo jewelry. It becomes this colour as result of glacial ice melting limestone, and leaving a suspension of rock dust in the water. He mixes more paint.

Any anxiety he harboured about how Pete and Catharine would react to his painting were immediately laid to rest when he found enough courage to revisit them.

Catharine opened the door to his knock. "Oh, it's you!"

"Yah. Is Pete Whyte in?"

"Sure. Pete!" she called up. "It's the Stoney friend George brought along last week."

The stairs creaked as Pete shuffled down from his new studio, wiping his hands on a paint-smeared rag. "Come on in, Frank!" He remembered Frank's name without hesitation. "Come in!"

They made him feel appreciated and relaxed; there seemed no risk in bringing out the subject of his visit.

"What's on your mind?" Pete asked.

"I brought some of my paintings. I want to show them to you."

He had to go back outside to fetch them from the car.

Pete studied them with keen interest. "I say! Come here, Catharine. Look at these!"

"They're really nice," she said. "They are really very good!"

The husband and wife exchanged looks of surprise, and then beamed at him. They studied the paintings in more detail.

"I think you may be interested in attending the Banff School of Fine Arts," Catharine said. "You have natural talent, and they would accept you, I think. They would teach you how to mix colours and improve your highlight effects."

His heart skipped beats. He'd attended the Morley Residential School when he was young, until grade eight. Now they would enrol him in an art school? The Banff School of Fine Arts? It would be like going to university, an advanced education normally reserved for those who have outstanding talent. His eyes shone at the prospect. No Stoney would have dared dream of such an opportunity.

"We may be able to enrol you for this summer," Pete announced. "I'll try and get you in. You could stay here for two or three nights if necessary."

"I'm working for the CPR," Sitting Wind admitted. "Section boss. It may be unwise to start something that will interfere with my job too much."

That had been the most fearful hurdle. It wasn't that he would be unable to break himself free of the work, but Kathleen and their children were now dependant on his pay cheque. Kathleen had built her bi-weekly routine on it. They would be unable to manage without money.

But Pete insisted. "Come back next Friday, after work, or on Saturday. We'll make some definite plans," he said.

They purchased one of his demonstration paintings, promising to keep it until he completed his courses, at which point he could assess his improvement. Just for the fun of it, they said.

"How are you mixing for this water, Frank?" His thoughts are interrupted by Adelle's shrill voice, from a gravel bench behind him. He is the only male in the course, out of fifteen students. He does not chum around too closely with any of the others; it's not proper for a married Stoney to make friends with other young ladies. But, the others find him fascinating: and Adelle is different, more of a tomboy.

"Jeesh. That looks all right. How did you mix to get that blue-green colour?" The gangly girl has ambled over and is studying the sketch over Sitting Wind's shoulder.

Pete's instructions sift through his mind again. "Let me show you how to achieve vibrant shades of green," the voice of experience explained in low tones. They were upstairs in his new studio. An assortment of other easels cradled paintings at various stages of completion. The walls were a mosaic of finished works, smartly framed. The only large window in the room was made to face north, Pete explained, so that direct sunlight could not enter and create lighting difficulties.

He'd erected an easel for Sitting Wind and provided a canvas. He explained things patiently, aware that his Indian pupil may not be familiar with painting jargon. Then he taught him that green, straight from the tube, does not correspond to the true colour of grass. By way of demonstration he took a little cerulean blue, a little yellow ochre, and a tiny bit of green. The result turned out quite dark, like avocado. It looked good on canvas.

"Now I don't mean that you should try to copy our paintings," he cautioned. "Simply paint what your eyes observe: whether through a window, or what you see in your mind.'' He taught Sitting Wind when to start, and when to quit with different components of a painting. ''Always do the sky first and work forward toward the foreground from there. The strong colours are used in the foreground.''

Sitting Wind's first painting was of the Vermilion Lakes with Mount Rundle behind them. He painted it from memory.

''I used cerulean blue and mixed it with yellow ochre,'' Sitting Wind responds to Adelle with self-assurance. ''And also some Venetian green. But not too much green. Be careful of that.''

Adelle passes the recipe around and soon others approach to assess the result for themselves. They laugh with one another about Sitting Wind's water, as if parading a joke past him. ''You make good water, Frank!'' they compliment him enthusiastically. ''Frank knows how to make the best water.''

He chuckles with them, although he does not immediately understand their humour.

The sun is fading rapidly now, clouds burgeoning. A vehicle has rumbled up the road from below and pulled short behind their parked bus. It is a jeep. Immediately Sitting Wind recognizes it as belonging to Pete and Catharine, and he waves enthusiastically for their attention. But they fail to notice him.

Hurriedly snatching up his canvas and easel he rushes down from the rocks, greeting them.

''Frank! How wonderful to meet you here. How is the painting progressing?'' Their eyes are fixed on the canvas. They wish to see his work. He raises it upright, boldly.

''That's fine work, Frank,'' they encourage him. ''You have improved immensely since you started last year.''

Sitting Wind's warm response is automatic, he needs no words. He has much for which to thank them. They have been his prime supporters from the day he met them.

''How are things going at Morley?'' Catharine's eyes have left the sketch and are penetrating his, searching his face. She is keenly interested in the people's day-to-day lives on the reserve, and has an uncanny ability to empathize. ''How are Kathleen and the kids?''

He recalls leaving them yesterday morning to return to Banff, Kathleen's eyes clinging to him wordlessly. She and the children have moved in with her mother, until he has finished his art courses for the summer. But he has applied with the Agent, to have a house built for themselves, their very own place. Now that he is Councillor he has more than a good chance.

''She is doing good.''

"Why don't you bring her up for a visit sometime? We'd love to have her. Tell her to bring the children, and the new baby."

He would like to do so. But where would they stay? They would have to drive back and forth on a weekend. Reverend Lonsdale's cabin is small, one room with one bed and a table to eat from: too small for his entire family. He cannot afford to rent a larger place.

"Maybe on a weekend we could come to your house, for tea," he suggests reluctantly.

Pete has wandered off to chat with the instructor, Mr. Phillips.

"Or better yet," she interrupts, sensing the cause of his hesitation. "Why don't you invite us to your place? We'll promise to come. There's nothing I would like more than for you to tell me all you know of Stoney history, to teach me what you know of the old ways, and show me places in your past."

Sitting Wind invites the artists. They agree to meet at Morley the following Saturday.

Morley

August, 1957

Having assessed the damage, Sitting Wind finds a rusty hammer and spade to begin the troublesome task of repair. Corral railings lie fanned out from a cracked post, to which they remain attached only tenuously, with twisted nails. Several rails are split. Another section has been rammed hard, with the result that its main support posts lean askew.

Today is Saturday: late afternoon. A day which turned sour already before dawn's soft light began to invade the eastern horizon behind Sitting Wind's cabin. A day which seemed to deteriorate as it wore on.

The cabin which he, Kathleen, and their two children now inhabit, is two rooms: a day-room featuring a large enamel wood stove with oven, and a night room which contains their beds. The exterior is asphalt felt, manufactured in patterns of large grey cinder blocks, and fixed to a wooden frame with short flat-headed nails. Its greatest attribute is that it is only a stone's throw from an abundance of fresh water tumbling down the Kananaskis River, toward the south-west end of Ozada Flats: the closest to the mountains one can reside and yet remain on reserve lands.

Kathleen elbowed his ribs painfully during the night.

"I think there's something going on with the horses!" she hissed with alarm in his ear.

At first his thoughts confused her words with visions of race-horses: muddled dreams.

"The dogs are barking and the horses are whinnying and restless," she said, shaking his shoulder. "Something is wrong." Instantly then, he also heard them: wood cracking, snapping. Sharp hooves stumbling frantically over railings. A frenzy of galloping.

By the time he arrived outside, rifle in hand under a starlit sky, the deed had been done. He could hear the bear woofing in trees beyond the clearing. A black bear probably. It had raided the meat-shed too: pulled out the deer carcass he had secured two evenings earlier. He returned to bed, knowing that he would need to restore order during the day.

During the middle of the morning, Catharine arrived. That was good, mind you. He was more than glad to see her. But the content of their various conversations had unsettled him. Now his life seems more confused, more unpredictable than ever. Just when he thought he was on the right track.

After wrenching the fallen railings from their leaning posts, Sitting Wind lays each end in turn across a stump, straightens the protruding nails with hammer claw, and then punches them back into position for re-use. With shovel and a section of pipe, he resets the loosened posts and firmly tamps gravel and soil at their bases. He might as well get the repairs done and over with, then return the horses to their pasture where they are more easily accessible for his occasional use.

"Pete begged me to apologize for him." Catharine started speaking before her feet touched ground, as she slid from the driver's seat of their jeep. "He has an unexpected visitor from Arizona, and has important business to attend to." Her arm was laden with a box of bakery tarts, and chocolates for them. "I insisted on the visit nevertheless. I knew you were counting on me, and I couldn't bear to disappoint you."

She shook his hand in greeting. Kathleen remained safely indoors, waiting to be called at the appropriate moment.

"Come on inside." Sitting Wind invited her tentatively.

The path toward the door suddenly seemed littered. Their fur-knotted dog wallowed timidly like a dusty pollywog against the wall. And her pups, whimpering, clambered up from somewhere beneath floor-boards to study, with small black eyes, the white stranger; they backed up clumsily at Catharine's approach. She laughed at them.

Kathleen made tea, and Catharine seemed to feel at home with the family, comfortable. She held Gerald in her lap, and kissed him playfully on the forehead.

Having re-attached the corral railings, Sitting Wind bridles one of the "quiet" horses, which has returned to feed from a slice of hay spread on the trampled ground. He approaches her broadside, gently. Although she lifts her head nervously, she permits him to slip the steel between her teeth, and the straps over her ears.

"Where are you going?" Kathleen calls from near the doorway. The blankets and sheets she washed after lunch are draped to dry over several bushes.

"Round up the horses!" he replies simply. "Before they wander off too far."

He is proud to have a bunch of horses. Whitemen come around to the reserve from time to time and try to purchase horses for the cannery in Calgary. But few people accept money. Most prefer to keep their stock, including wild and unusable mustangs, because they are a symbol, a lingering reminder of an active wilderness life which once provided essential meaning to the old culture.

Heaving his right leg up and over, he rolls into the hollow of her back. The remainder of the herd has likely taken cover somewhere in aspen stands upstream along the river, depending on the course taken by the bear. He directs his mount toward the water, scanning the ground for bear tracks. Although unlikely at this season, it's not impossible that it was a grizzly.

"It's a beautiful spot for raising a family," Catharine remarked as they surveyed the damaged corral. She'd wanted to see the evidence for herself before he started the repairs. She wished to see their on-reserve living environment. "So much space for growing up. So much freedom."

Kathleen had remained in the cabin with the children.

Sitting Wind considered her words. Massive power-lines crossed his field of vision, breaking the vista of mountains into wavy slices. They passed directly over fields on the river's other side, where his whiteman friend Alvin Guinn had recently built a luxurious guest ranch.

"I guess you're right," he replied, too politely agreeable at first. Then, after some thought he felt compelled to add, "But, in another way, the people feel cooped up here. Maybe it's different for you white people, since you don't live on a reserve." Briefly he assessed Catharine's reaction. But she was silent, absorbed his words.

"For us Indians it used to be different," he continued more boldly.

Catharine turned to face him directly.

"What I mean," he said, "is that when I was younger I used to live in tepees at Rabbit Lake: with my grandparents, and my uncle, Josiah. It was better during that time."

"I understand what you feel." Catharine spoke quietly after a silence. "The situation is sad."

At the water's edge, Sitting Wind is relieved to find bear tracks in the moist clay. The offender crossed at this point; therefore the horses will not have been driven too far. Allowing his eyes to follow the flow of water downstream, he studies the distant bridge over the Trans-Canada. Catharine's jeep will have crossed it half an hour earlier. She could be half way back to Banff already.

Pulling his horse's head sharply left, he begins the task of system-atically checking riverside aspen stands. They will be in there somewhere, hiding in the cover.

"You see," he'd elaborated to her, "in the old days, when Treaty was made, our reserve was a safe place to which people could return after hunting and gathering treks. The mountains were like our backyard, where we would be busy for a season harvesting our food, and finally we would come home to the reserve as if it were a warm fireplace to tide us through cold winters. But it's completely different now. Today, our backyard is taken away: our source of food. And that's why our house is now a prison. Every time we step out through the door we are met with a heavy choking air of whitemen's laws and whitemen's disapproving scowls. That's how it's different today."

"Well said," she said as though thinking out loud. "And from the deepest part of your heart."

They sat in silence for a time, Catharine nibbling on a culm of grass. The dog came grovelling at Sitting Wind's feet, licking his fingertips solicitously. He ignored the dog. It was then that she posed the most disquieting questions.

"One thing puzzles me," she said. "I don't understand how the Christian God fits in with the old ways. I don't mean to discourage you from believing in God, you understand. I'm simply curious. If you feel that whitemen have slowly imprisoned you within your reserve by taking away your food supply, how is it that you believe in whitemen's God?"

He was taken aback. What could he say that would justify his leanings? He felt trapped. With gentle force he pushed the dog aside and twisted his boot heel into the dust. Did it ever matter how God was addressed? Are not all gods the same in the end? As long as there is peace and understanding: sympathy, empathy, consideration. He merely wishes that whitemen would understand Indians, be patient, be considerate, be respectful of them as fellow human beings. Is that not what God represents?

When she sensed his discomfort, she backtracked. "Pay no attention to my silly questions," she said lightly. "I do this all the time. You must understand that I am intensely interested in everything to do with Indians. I'm not only interested in your handicrafts: it's much more than that. I want to know your history, your culture, your religion, everything."

Her tone became more serious. "I'm on your side," she continued, meticulously emphasizing the word 'your' as Mrs. Leopard had used to do when he was at the Residential School. "I believe that you have become imprisoned in the manner you described. I believe that your old way of life deserves much more consideration than what has been given by whitemen. And I want to help you in any way I can. I mean that. I want to help you.''

''You have already helped me a great deal,'' he replied. ''I will never be able to repay you for helping me in art, and getting me into the Banff School of Fine Arts.''

''But that's only a small beginning.'' Catharine pressed on. ''There's a much greater work to be done. Work that can be accomplished only through the chief and councils: such as fighting for your rights under the Treaty. That's what I mean. I will help with that, too. I want to assist you in your work as a band councillor.''

Suddenly the horses are before him, within a small clearing, their eyes and ears pricked up to the horse and rider. Sitting Wind's horse neighs in greeting. He begins a wide circle around to position himself behind them for the ambling drive back to the corral at his cabin.

''What should I do then?'' Sitting Wind had wondered out loud to Catharine.

''The very first thing,'' she responded firmly, ''is to respect your traditional culture. Don't be ashamed of it. Don't apologize for it. In many ways it is far superior to the whiteman's culture. You should stand by the old values.''

He was shocked. Her words affected him as if they were a reprimand. They were not unlike Grandma's words, spoken during her last days, warning him to stick with the old ways. Had she implied that he has been wandering down the wrong road after all?

With warmth in his eyes he smiled at her. Catharine understands him. She understands Indians. She is a friend.

''I want to tell you something,'' he said carefully. ''Something which I thought I would never tell anyone again.''

She scrutinized his expression expectantly. He seemed forlorn, resigned.

''Remember you once asked me about my Indian name? Where it came from?''

She nodded.

''I'd like to tell you about it now.''

That's how he came to tell her the stories which Grandma had repeated to him in the past: of his mother Mary, of Beaver Woman, of Mountain Walker, of the special song given by the powerful Wind Spirit. And he didn't stop there. Suddenly all his past experiences, experiences he had slowly learned to suppress, boiled to the surface and longed to be laid out for this friend. He told her everything in a long, rambling monotone, as if making a confession: of Banff Indian Days, of the Residential School, of rodeos, of Joe Poucette and their days in the army, of how the elders spoke out against war because they wanted to preserve the sacred Treaty of peace.

Catharine listened as if in a trance, enthralled by every visual detail, as if by his telling each could become a personal experience.

''You should use your spiritual name,'' she encouraged him before climbing back into her jeep. ''Sign it to your paintings.''

''Okay,'' he replied. ''I will.''

Trans-Canada Highway
May, 1962

"Which way you headed, man?"

A youthful hitchhiker's blood-shot eyes framed in a rusty beard are pushed through the half-open passenger door of Sitting Wind's GMC pickup, which he has pulled onto the Trans-Canada's shoulder. The young man's words are punctuated by gasps of breath, caused by his sudden dash. A girl was catching up behind him, hobbling under the weight of an army ruck-sack.

"I'm only going to Canmore, but it's better than nothin', anyways. Come on in." Sitting Wind's welcome is almost apologetic.

"Hey, great. That's cool, man. Thanks a million." The girl has caught up now, long hair reaching below shoulders, bunched, unkept. Throwing their gear into the open back they clamber up into the seat beside him.

"We're heading out to the coast: Vancouver Island," he pants, adjusting their cramped legs as the door slams them into place. They are wearing wool shirts, she a long cotton print skirt which she hauls in close to her legs so as not to tangle with the floor shift. A scruffy young cat curls into her lap: it could have been white once. They could almost be Indians, Sitting Wind notes, the way they are dressed: she with beads around her ankle, dusty bare feet in sandals, and long earrings like hoops. Gypsies maybe.

For a moment silence returns — some cultural distance rising between them — as Sitting Wind levers into first gear and lurches forward onto pavement again. He enjoys stopping for hitchhikers, wondering to what exciting places they are headed and what strange places they have left behind. Whitemen are different in that respect: they feel less obligation to remain with their families. They leave and travel around freely, fearlessly, anywhere.

It is well into the morning, spring. The Morley Flats circle by, recently become alive with soft colours of small flowers thrusting up through gravelly soil after the April rains. As the truck gathers speed, rows of fence posts rattle by the windows. In pastures enclosed by the

162

fences, they observe several bands of horses, young foals and fillies with long vacuum snouts arched under their mothers' hind legs, or stretched out on bare ground within protective shadows of their mares who stand over them patiently.

"Like, this is a real neat place, man," the burly hitchhiker says with a wide grin. "You live around here somewhere?"

"Yup. In fact this is my reserve we're on right now," Sitting Wind says with a smile. "I'm a Stoney Indian."

"Wow, man. Would I like to live in a place like this." His eyes momentarily address Sitting Wind's, as if truly expecting that Sitting Wind may offer him permission to stay and set up house here. Through the cracked windshield the girl is scanning contours of hills which unfold into the base of Mount Yamnuska's steep cliffs and, more distantly, into mountains of the upper Ghost River.

"So, what do you do around here?" he asks, still trying to assess for himself the extent of local opportunity.

"I'm a chief now," Sitting Wind states proudly. "That's about it. It's a pretty tough job." As soon as the words leave his lips he remembers his art. "And I'm an artist too. I paint oils. You may have heard of me. I sell paintings all over the world: Sitting Wind. That's my name, Sitting Wind. But being a chief sure keeps me busy."

He was voted in as chief of the Bearspaw Band over a year ago: March 10, 1961. The election had originally been in January but there was a tie vote between him and old Johnny Bearspaw. The people elected him in a rerun. There is need for younger blood, some argued.

"Hey, all right! Cherilyn paints too." The gyspy grins at his companion, wedged between them. "When we were at Yorkville she started doing natural scenes: flowers, and beautiful people." The girl nods earnestly in agreement.

When his first term as councillor was completed in 1959, the people wanted him to run immediately again as councillor; some even wanted him to run as chief. He withdrew his nomination for several reasons. "I think I prefer to be painting and maybe a regular job on the side," he explained to Kathleen. "I was making more money before, when I was with the CPR"

On top of that there was his father.

"You're way too young to be on Council," his father John had warned him. He sat in a chair opposite Sitting Wind on the other side of the cabin. His frame was slight, like Sitting Wind's own, and he had aged. As John nervously wiped a slender, almost frail, hand over his left ear, Sitting Wind was stricken by how his short-clipped hair was now richly peppered with coarse grey.

It was the first time he had ever come to Morley to visit his Stoney son. He'd come all the way from Hobbema, in order to relay his sentiments. "I'm very concerned about you going ahead with this nomination. If you continue, your hair will turn white long before you are old enough to have white hair."

"But if people ask for me," Sitting Wind threw back at him, "should I turn them down? They will begin to suspect I'm afraid of something." Although he basically respected his father, he continued to be like a stranger to him, and Sitting Wind was not afraid of him, of counteracting his advice. What he wished to impress upon him was that people seemed to need his help and guidance.

He went along with his father on that occasion. But he decided to let his nomination stand during this most recent election. Withdrawal of his name during the previous election had hurt him. The people expressed grave disappointment and made him feel guilty of lacking desire to fight for them. It became clear that the Band's need for his help was urgent.

His call to serve on Council became like an inescapable call to duty: to war. To say no again would be tantamount to admitting cowardice, defeat, and weakness. They need him now. They are tired of being controlled by a non-Stoney government, manipulated and taken for granted by non-Stoney government officials. And he can count on Catharine and other friends to stand by his side in case of trouble.

Additional persuasion came from a most unexpected source. "He wants to see you real bad!" they said. "He's dying."

Enoch Baptiste's relatives were begging him. Enoch Baptiste had always disliked Sitting Wind. "You're just a Cree; you don't belong with the Stoneys." This is what he used to say. But now, three days before his death he was begging to see him.

Sitting Wind made his way to the hospital reluctantly, and found the old man slipping in and out of consciousness. What could he want with me now? Sitting Wind wondered, as he opened a heavy glass door into that world of chloroform, ether, and white silence. The old man's eyes fluttered open and stared at him, focussing, recognizing him, from the creased hollow of his pillow.

"I requested to see you because I have news for you from above."

Sitting Wind nodded, bracing for a final derision, a last spiteful smear before Enoch's passage into the land of journeys.

"I'm sorry for hating you all these years," he said, his breath coming in gasps. "I must make peace with you. I now realize that you stand in a spotlight which shines down from above. You are the only one in this light. Darkness is all around, and people in darkness dishonour you with rumours and gossip. I have seen this. It was told to me and I am instructed to relay this to you.''

For a moment his attention lapsed, his eyes falling heavy, but he caught himself and forced them open again, straining to complete this transfer. ''Please forgive me, Sitting Wind. I only hated you because I didn't know what I know now, what I have been told in a vision.'' Tears were rolling down his cheeks although there were no crying sounds. ''I know now that you shall keep on travelling,'' he continued, ''on the path upon which you travel already, and the Great Spirit will be with you. The Great Spirit will be with you, hear me? It will be a tough road, but you must persist because the Great Spirit will be with you. Forgive me. I was unaware that you are honoured from above.'' The powerful words whirled through Sitting Wind's memory for days afterwards, tugging at almost-forgotten promises once made by the Wind. Promises of greatness. Of leadership.

''I would be painting a lot more,'' Sitting Wind says, glancing at the youths with a heavy sigh, ''if the people hadn't elected me to be their chief. This is the only hindrance to my art, you might say. They need me. That's the hard part of it. They can't seem to do without me.''

The most vexing problem, which persists just beneath the surface of most council deliberations, is that hardly anyone has a job. Perhaps Band members were able to keep themselves more occupied with jobs in times past or simply tried harder, having more hope. Maybe they have become more inclined to give up trying, and have resigned themselves to living day by day without interest in their futures. Or are there really fewer job opportunities available than there used to be?

That's why he was willing to make this sacrifice, he explained to Kathleen. The people wish to make changes, to get out from under control of white government. He may be able help. He has experience dealing with people off the reserve; he has served in the army, has been a boxer, has graduated from the Banff School of Fine Arts because, as his art instructor Mr. Phillips said, laying a hand on his shoulder, ''There's not a whole lot more you can learn here, Frank. You know everything now!''

The hikers rearrange their legs, becoming more relaxed since the truck has settled into a comfortable rumbling, cruising speed. ''What sort of things do you do if you're a chief?'' the girl asks, a half question, furrowing her forehead into deep arcs.

Sitting Wind ponders it. After picking up diapers in Canmore for their two-year-old baby, Karen, he will drive back to Morley for a council meeting at the Agency office. Last week they went to Calgary, a delegation of Treaty Seven chiefs all wearing their official chiefs' uniforms with brass buttons, and they voiced their concerns about the federal election. A few years ago the government passed a law permitting Indians to vote in Canadian elections. But the elders are deeply suspicious that this may be a plot to weaken and eventually eliminate Treaty promises. They are fighting for their Treaty rights, with help from the Alberta Indian Association.

"Well, there's quite a few different things involved," he begins. "I have to look after my people, especially those who are short of money or food. And then we fight for Indian rights too. Treaty rights. It's a big job. Sometimes I even need to fly to Ottawa, or drive to Edmonton and Calgary for meetings."

With quiet exclamations to one another, the two passengers admire the towering cliffs which are gradually enclosing the truck and its occupants, swallowing up their ribbon of pavement. The vehicle's springs are rigid, and hard rubber tires skip rhythmically over regular pavement seams. The Bow River, awaiting a swell of run-off, meanders easily through a gorge of rock bluffs and gravel bars on their right.

"As anywhere in Canada, we Indians usually don't have much education. I guess you may have noticed that by now," Sitting Wind says with a sigh. His companions are only semi-attentive. "That's why we have to depend on the white government for our Treaty rights, to help us survive. We could survive all right if there were enough hunting areas. But that's the problem: our hunting lands are running out."

The girl is stroking the cat's dusty fur. Her bracelet is silver bangles.

Sitting Wind's mind reviews a heated meeting which erupted last month when the federal election was debated by elders and council. Some of the younger council members like Eddie Hunter, Bert Wildman, and himself, are more inclined to try discussing issues with the government rather than being too quickly suspicious and defensive. But elders' arguments carry the weight of traditional respect and experience. Their arguments cannot be thwarted.

Kathleen's father, Johnny Chiniquay, stood up in the meeting, supported by his cane. Band members who were lined up against an interior wall of the Agency Office kept their eyes fixed to the floor, pondering various points of view.

The venerated elder had opened the meeting with a humble prayer; his faltering Stoney words lifting and falling musically like a chant. He'd called upon the Great Spirit to give guidance and prosperity to 'my people'. That prayer reminded Sitting Wind how well Catharine understood Indians. She perceived the essential role of humility in their way of life. It was a value to which he himself, he suddenly realized with alarm, was gradually becoming immune, blind.

These elders have dignity. The old ways have dignity. They command respect. Catharine showed sensitivity to the essence of old ways, and helped him re-align his own perspective. It was Johnny Chiniquay's father, Kathleen's grandfather, who signed the sacred Treaty in 1877.

Now, the elder's tone was icy, embittered by injustice. "A lawyer told us that we have been given the privilege to vote as Canadians. But I don't think anything a whiteman has given us in times past has turned out for our benefit. You people who desire to vote, go ahead and vote. Override us elders, and then you will have your way."

"Lawyers have discussed this thoroughly," countered young Eddie Hunter with some impatience. He is more educated and is a good friend of John Laurie, who helped start the Indian Association of Alberta. "They feel you will have a voice if you vote through representation. They have already said you'll not lose any Treaty rights. Other reserves have been told, after checking carefully, that they will not lose their Treaty rights."

But elders resisted more and more as the meeting progressed.

"That's cool, man. All right!" The bearded youth beams with enthusiasm. He is referring to the mountains and the river, and the lime factory washed in white chalk against the valley's opposite side.

"Do Treaty rights.... Do they.... Is that what you mean by hunting wild animals and that kind of thing?" asks the girl, gesturing with her wrists.

"Well, I guess you could say it means survival sort of," replies Sitting Wind. Mr. Hardy used to have a copy of the Treaty tacked to the Agency wall: a sacred promise to allow hunting, trapping, and fishing forever on unoccupied Crown land.

"I have said sour grapes." Jake Rabbit said.

The Agent was sunk into his chair, tilted backwards on two legs against the wall, sucking long on a cigarette between thumb and browned index finger.

"In the past," Jake Rabbit said, "we owned the country. Then whitemen came and made us friendly, and then made Treaty for our rights, promising that no one would be able to break this sacred Treaty. Now, if we are going to vote, the government should first tell us how they are going to look after us."

Old Isaac Rollinmud stirred from his thoughts, gnarled walking stick resting on his lap. His voice wavered when he spoke. "When Treaty was signed nobody spoke English, and we simply believed the *waseejew* (whitemen). We speak English now, yet some of you still believe the whitemen. We are not well educated in whitemen's ways, but I feel they have baited a trap, and in the future they will surprise us again. The smart fish does not take a bait at first sight.''

Enoch Rider nodded his head, wanting to interrupt, to elaborate. ''Chief Bearspaw laid down his weapons in 1877 and accepted Treaty on the promise that whitemen's government would protect us as long as the sun shines and the rivers flow. If Council now decides to reject the vote, then I will feel very happy. The Montana Indians have told me that when they accepted the vote, it was the beginning of their end. First their land was immediately quartered, and eventually when they became desperate they sold what little land remained. Now they are nothing. We must be progressive to make a better living. I have grandchildren and I hope that, as they grow up, they too will be against whitemen in every way possible. Myself, I'm not scared because I have not long to live; but I fear for our future generations. Some of you have fallen for this trap. I warn you: *waseejew* means 'terrible looking'.''

Johnny Bearspaw agreed. ''We should all refuse to vote. I feel that the government is trying to force our reserve system out of existence. I mean our hunting rights, fishing rights, and our freedom to roam forests and plains. Whitemen have to work because they have to pay taxes. But not us. I prefer our own way of living.''

The Agent made no comment, merely scribbled in a minute book, his face betraying no thoughts. Meanwhile, Band members clamored for answers, for trust, for security.

Why do whitemen continue to back us into cliffs. Why? Why? Why? Sitting Wind is convinced that the people need him. They depend on him. If he could only think of a way to help them more. More dramatically.

''I guess you must be going on a holiday, then,'' Sitting Wind inquires, attempting to wrest his thoughts away from problems which seem impossible to resolve.

''Hey man, we're thinking of findin' ourselves a place to live, you know,'' replies the beard. ''Some friends of ours back in Toronto, they've got some other friends near Granville Island where we can crash for a bit, and then we're gonna find a place somewhere on the west coast, maybe up on Denman or Hornby Island. What we need is a tepee, or something. We could live in a tepee until we get enough bread together for buildin' our own pad.''

He has brought out a crumpled bag of tobacco and is rolling a cigarette. ''Care for a smoke?'' he asks.

''Sure!'' replies Sitting Wind. ''Maybe you could roll one for me too.''

The cat has uncoiled and, with dainty forepaws on the dashboard, is cautiously investigating the threatening mountains, her nose dabbing the windshield.

''Say, you wouldn't know where I could get hold of a tepee around here?'' The young man phrases his question directly.

''Not really. We usually make our own; our Agent buys the canvas in town.''

''Right on, man. Well, we'll be all right. It'd be too much to carry around anyway, you know. As long as we can make it to Vancouver with three bucks, we'll be all right.'' They light up, smoke columns circling the interior. ''Three bucks left, and that's it,'' he repeats almost cynically, grinning.

The valley has opened slightly now as their truck has passed through the Gap and approaches Deadman's Flats. As they motor along, Sitting Wind scans the small meadows passing on their right, and the larger ones on their left, leading up the reaches of Wind Creek. He saw elk and deer down low here last month, scouring for the earliest spring greens sprouting skyward through the soil. He used to camp here years ago, trap beaver in late winter. Indian Flats is on the other side, across Mnee Thnay.

''A sacred area to be used only for emergency survival,'' a medicine man had told Grandpa. And Grandma sat there quietly that night, when a coyote howled and the pup whined.

''We never needed any money in the old days,'' Sitting Wind observes casually. ''That's the trouble with our young people today, they have forgotten our old Stoney ways and they don't know how to survive anymore.''

''Hey man, like we're from Toronto,'' the beard laughs. ''Money city. If you know how to survive without money, man, a cat like me ought to be takin' lessons from you. Know what I mean?'' His grinning face has turned directly into Sitting Wind's. ''What I mean is, if I could get by with no money I'd be doin' it right now. But a man's got to eat, you know.''

Sitting Wind recalls the patient instructions of Uncle Josiah. ''That's not the way you dig them,'' he scoffed, pushing Sitting Wind aside. ''First you have to scrape some rocks, like this, and then you push the stick in deep to cut the bottoms of the carrots.'' After several tries he was able to pull up long carrots, sweet and succulent. He carried some back with him for Grandma, who gummed them with her broken teeth.

''I'll show you what to eat then,'' Sitting Wind offers suddenly, almost eagerly, withdrawing his foot from the accelerator and braking to a stop near Deadman's Flats.

"Hey man, don't go out of your way. I was just kidding. We'll be okay. We'll be just fine."

"No, I'll show you in the field here," Sitting Wind insists. "You can find food here which is free, such as we Stoney Indians used to survive on every day, in the old days. I'll point some out for you, and if you eat them you won't need to spend any money at all."

The girl's skirt unfolds like wash on a line, billowing gently as they waltz down an incline into the meadow. Scanning the soil eagerly for familiar immature purple stalks, leaves not yet fully unfolded, Sitting Wind feels momentarily young again, his legs lifting lightly like young deer, across pebbles and hummocks.

"Look for purple stems," he lectures enthusiastically. "They taste real good."

They follow his eyes closely, overwhelmed by the spectrum of emergent life like a carpet beneath their feet. They dig like hungry grizzlies on hillsides, laughing and probing with sticks under a noon sun.

Sitting Wind shows them wild carrots, and then white willows near the river. "You can eat these any time. They will fill you up, and you won't get hungry for a hundred or even five hundred miles!" He beams.

They take some, stuff them in their packs.

"Anytime you stop, simply search for some of these natural foods. By the time you get to Vancouver, you'll still have your three dollars."

He chuckles like a child. It was easy in the old days. So much simpler.

"Hey man. I don't know how to thank you. You really know what you're doin'!" The hefty gypsy says it sincerely, suddenly hugging him across the truck seat, cheek to cheek like his Cree relatives did when he went to meet his father. "That's some trip, man. I'm sure we'll never forget this little ride or the stuff you showed us."

Before he can recover composure, the girl pecks Sitting Wind on the cheek too, the cat squashed silently to her lap. They slide out into the intersection, lifting their packs from the rear box.

"Peace, brother! If there were more people like you, our world would be different, man!" he shouts, waving through an open window as the truck lurches away.

I'll be late for this meeting, Sitting Wind realizes, as he noses eastward. Drove them all the way to Eisenhower Junction, teaching them Stoney ways of survival. The old Indian ways. Recollecting ancient stories which Grandpa told.

"It's okay," he assures himself. "They'll have to put up with me arriving on 'Indian time'. If they have started, that is."

Lake Minnewanka

Indian woman making dry-meat

Sitting Wind's aunt, Mrs. Tom Kaquitts, scraping a hide

Stoney hunter in winter attire

Sitting Wind's Uncle: George McLean

Johnny Chiniquay's Cabin

Sketch of Kathleen

*Sitting Wind in chief's uniform, as issued by
the Department of Indian Affairs*

Sitting Wind wearing Treaty coat

Sitting Wind as Sitting Bull

Sitting Wind: portrait of the artist

Peter and Catharine Whyte, Banff

Home of Peter and Catharine Whyte

Painting by Sitting Wind

Painting by Sitting Wind

Sitting Wind painting in his studio

Sitting Wind at home in his craft workshop

Sitting Wind and Kathleen, today

Ottawa
February 25, 1974

How could they possibly know already that he is in Ottawa? Sitting Wind marvels. The words of a message which awaited his late afternoon arrival at the Townhouse Motel's front desk are hand-scrawled with ball-point. He rereads them carefully, collapsed with exhaustion upon the yellow bedspread.

February 25/74. Stoney Indian Chief Frank Kaquitts: Please attend meeting at the Land Claims Commissioner's Office tomorrow at 9:30 am, Parliament Buildings, Block D, Room 121.

February 25. He's forty-nine today. Forty nine. Almost fifty!

Of more prolonged interest are the words of salutation which arouse an ominous mixture of both pride and fear. "Stoney Indian Chief," it says. Not simply chief of one of the Stoney Bands, but Stoney Indian Chief. Whoever left this message must have advance intelligence of who he is, and know that he is to spend a few days in the country's capital.

True, to an unacquainted outsider who has not seen his photo in the *Calgary Herald*, the new, celebrated title may not mean much. One would need to know of the nagging internal problems of three historically separate Stoney Bands, at loggerheads virtually since the day they were herded together onto one undivided reserve almost a hundred years ago.

In terms of internal politics and prestige, his new title epitomizes the pinnacle of achievement. In fact, it is beyond any pinnacle known to date, because never before has one person been appointed grand Chief of all three Bands, of all the Stoney people. Who would ever have dared dream that he, Sitting Wind, would be the first? The first Stoney Indian Chief.

Following years of debate, a referendum held last November finally approved amalgamation of the three groups. And then, for good or for ill, Sitting Wind was elected. It was no marginal victory, either, but rather an overwhelming majority: he received more than twice the number of votes of either of the other two contestants.

"My most sincere congratulations, Frank!" Catharine exclaimed over the telephone that same night. "The people could not have made a better choice."

However, now that almost six weeks have slipped by since the victory, the initial bliss has given way to less splendid realities. Allowing the message to slip from his tired fingers onto the bedside table, he wonders with a wrench of concern where this chieftainship will lead. He hasn't been sleeping regularly. His eyes feel worn and dry. He allows them to pass along the plaster-sprayed ceiling over his head, the flat beige walls, the deftly framed prints of orange and brown maple trees, centered perfectly between the ends of the veneered dresser, and screwed tight to the wall so no one will steal them.

There is another side to being the one and only: being the only one. The one who is alone, and on unfamiliar territory. There's no one else to rely on when a situation becomes too complex, too difficult. It has become apparent that the course of his current fate turns precariously on people's whims. Initially, everyone looked up to him for the answers; now, when some answers surface more slowly than people's patience would like, he has noticed eyes too readily turning hollow, restless, critical.

He cannot provide all the answers, certainly not in the short term. The problems are like hornets around a crushed nest; angry, disarrayed, confused. If he could only be given the confidence that the people would stand strong beside him until everyone became more accustomed to there being only one chief, then he would feel so much stronger. Instead, they seem bent on forcing him into a posture of defence.

Rumours back home are being circulated that he is too educated, too much like a whiteman who does not understand or care about the old ways. Someone even criticized his hair: "Why does he not have long hair like an Indian?"

Attitudes seem to change so easily, within so short a period of time.

Shutting his eyes to the glare which is erasing the detail of ceiling and wall textures, Sitting Wind recalls his victory speech. "My Indian brothers," he began, his words ringing. "It seems we are now one Stoney Tribe instead of three Bands." A reporter from the *Herald* was flashing his camera, sharply, from different angles. "And you have put me in the saddle, which I can see is going to make for a very tough ride. I can tell you straight: this horse you have placed me on has had a habit of wanting to go in several different directions at the same time. Maybe it will refuse to listen to me." The image of a horse reminded him of the day he'd tried to ride old Wildeyes at the Residential

School: the day they tied him into the Agency saddle. He chuckled.

"Just the same, you have done me a great honour by making me the chief of all three Bands. Although I am not one to boast about it. I will follow your wishes. I will help my people and see to your daily needs, and your problems.

"The way I see it, being under only one chief instead of three was easy to achieve. But, becoming one tribe instead of three bands is going to be difficult. This is not accomplished by a simple referendum and vote. That was merely a first step. The only way we will become members of one tribe is for each one of us Stoney people to *think* as a member of one tribe. To stop thinking of himself or herself as a member of this band or that band: to start thinking of ourselves only as Stoneys, all of us the same."

But his best efforts were not sufficient. Disagreements over the election results surfaced almost immediately after the votes were counted. The same malicious, pre-election arguments were recklessly unsheathed and brandished, even in council meetings: if they changed to a one-chief system it would be tantamount to tampering with the basis of the Treaty, and this would threaten to undermine the sacred Treaty rights.

"I think the best plan, in the circumstances, is to request a letter from Indian Affairs Minister Chretien," Catharine advised him by telephone. "See that photocopies are posted around the reserve, so everyone can clearly see that the Treaty will not be affected."

Now he is here. Obtaining such a letter is his Ottawa mission.

The several rums-and-cokes he had on the plane continue to mollify his deepest fear, that in the end he may be forced to step down. It is a fear that feels like an angry grizzly within his chest, straining to tear free in rage and frustration should the fear prove real.

He has his family and friends at least, and they support him. In addition to Catharine, there are his friends Bill Elliot and his wife, Ruth. Ruth and Kathleen visit one another. And there is Kathleen herself, her days filled from dawn to dusk with the youngest of their children: Vera Ann is six-and-a-half, and Bernadette is four-and-a-half. The family is happy with the new four bedroom house they received three years ago.

"How can you remain tolerant and patient with all these rumours people are spreading around?" Kathleen's aged father challenged him last week. But Sitting Wind was already cautious about betraying his innermost feelings. He merely assured John Chiniquay that he pays no attention to rumours and gossip because they are wrong: lies. He cannot afford to afford to pay attention to these things. A person must be protected by this pride. It's the only way.

"As Chief, am I not expected to visit people in need, sometimes also separated young women?" he responded almost defiantly. "Is it not my job to counsel? Even if it generates rumours? This is what my Grandpa Ben once described to me as the role of a chief, and I have always tried to follow his advice."

"I hear anger behind your voice. But my words were not in criticism, son," Kathleen's father countered. "I only stand in admiration of your strength and endurance at this time of great unrest among the people. But I warn you that even these traits may not be enough. It is proper and just for a chief's mind to be concerned full-time for his people, and not for his personal needs or gain. I warn you also that people can be unpredictable; they can suddenly turn on you like a bull, with hostility, jealousy, maliciousness. I have seen it during my life."

"Perhaps you have some advice for me then," Sitting Wind said, offering a tentative invitation. "You are my father-in-law, and you are old and more experienced in the traditional ways. I would be honoured to listen with respect to how chiefs in the old Stoney way conducted themselves. The truth is, I feel in need of your help."

There followed a pause first, during which Sitting Wind watched the old man tug a snuff tin from his plaid shirt breast pocket, tap it, and place a pinched wad behind his lower lip. The couch's upholstered armrest was soiled like rubbed bark; crumbs of past meals lay accumulated in folds of its disheveled blanket throw-cover. The living room window, overlooking the flat of the Chiniki Village area, was finger-painted with grimy hands of barefoot grandchildren. He could hear echoes of their play bouncing down the empty hallway from a distant bedroom, and visualized their polished black eyes and tightly wrapped Pampers.

In the distance, pressed by the Trans-Canada's four lanes of pavement into a knoll of scrawny aspen and pine, his eyes fell upon the original Chiniquay cabin where Kathleen was born. An irregular flow of traffic criss-crossed the face of the cabin. He used to come there and court her. Once, after a dinner, they became husband and wife there. This same old man on the couch before him built that cabin, made decisions within its rough timbers, reviewing elements of a sinewed life and assessing the graveness of consequences.

"Today," his father-in-law began at last, "chiefs have been known to boast publicly, saying, 'I am the chief'. This is not right. Traditional chiefs of long ago would have been hard to distinguish from other Band members. They were ordinary men, although they had power with rocks, with animals with everything: and had great wealth. They had power given by the Spirits, and this was evident from the many scalps they were able to secure.

"In the old days a chief was brave in battle and impartial in his favour to people under his authority. He was concerned especially for the weak, the disadvantaged, and poor. He was quick to encourage a peaceful settlement, and slow to become angry. But when provoked he showed no fear of adversaries. That, my son, is what a chief should be like, and from observing your strength so far, I think you already know what makes a good chief. I pray that your endurance will be as great as required."

The elder's words were heartening, and they have power even now as he lies limp, motivation draining over realities like warm water poured on ice. At that moment, with Johnny Chiniquay, everything seemed suddenly to come together, the whole progression of his life heading after all toward the grand destiny of Ganutha Inghay — Sitting Wind — as it was foretold by Mountain Walker. What greater strength or motivation could he wish for?

The recollection of those sentiments revives a sense of purpose. He has made no mistake. This was undoubtedly the sudden turn in his life that Grandma predicted prior to her death. Look at him now — born small and unimportant, forty nine years ago, fighting continuously against odds throughout life: and surviving. More than surviving. He has gained much experience in the process. It was all meant to be this way. Why should he give up, ever?

Fist rubbing sleep from his eyes, Sitting Wind sits up on the edge of the bed. His watch reads 6:27. Time to find a place to eat. The anticipation of a hot-beef sandwich and a beer heartens him.

"I guess Ottawa is what you could call an office-hours city, eh?" Sitting Wind observes to the Checker taxi driver as they coursed smartly through traffic early next morning. "It seems that every person has a job and a time schedule."

As the driver makes no apparent effort to respond, Sitting Wind continues his observations privately. Hurried columns of people shuttle along sidewalks and corridors, into tall buildings, where they will break up into smaller groups bumping up elevator shafts, up into rooms with desks.

The most remarkable thing, he thinks, is the sense of purpose that appears to drive each individual, the concentration and personal dedication to some apparently important daily chore to be performed. Each person cherishes a small bit of distinct purpose, somehow fitting into a whole, like ants contributing to the colony, caravans hauling in tiny fragments of soil litter to patch and develop the nest.

The taxi has pulls away before a wake of lingering monoxide fumes, leaving him standing on the winter sidewalk in front of the Parliament Buildings. "A little on the blustery side, with sixty percent chance of flurries," the TV weatherman said apologetically this morning from the color screen as Sitting Wind cinched his belt buckle to the appropriate notch. None too warm for his blue down jacket and fur-lined gloves. Now, exposed to the air, his thin cowboy hat pulled down tightly offers scant cover from the cold settling into his clipped black hair.

Two security guards flanking the main entrance demand identification. Sitting Wind explains himself and his purpose, and is happy to note by their friendly nods that this year they seem to be expecting him.

He innocently attempted to set up a meeting once, several years earlier. "My name is Frank Kaquitts," he'd said. "And I thought I might as well meet with the prime minister for a few questions."

It was his first experience as a Band chief, and he had always envisioned chiefs and leaders anywhere in the country to be like buddies, on first name bases. The telephone of his motel room had a greasy film, and the mouthpiece was perfumed by a previous room occupant.

"Frank Kaquitts. ... I'm a Stoney from Morley." He frowned at framed daisies on the wall as the receptionist responded with puzzlement, uncertainty. Perhaps she needed more information.

"I'm in Ottawa until tomorrow morning so I thought we might be able get together for just a short meeting this afternoon, if that's all right with him." A further pause, more questions, hesitation.

"... Frank Kaquitts. I'm on the council. ...No, no. I'm an Indian; that's why I thought he might be interested in meeting with me."

"...Morley. Alberta."

She gently explained that the prime minister was in a cabinet meeting this afternoon. Perhaps Frank would like to meet with the Assistant Deputy Minister of Indian Affairs. Impressed with the length of his title, Sitting Wind did not hesitate.

"... Yes. That sounds pretty good. ...Two o'clock? ...Could you say that again, please. I better write it down, you know. Or I might forget." He put it carefully in his notebook. "Thank you very much!"

The clap of his shoes on the geometrically patterned granite floor echoes against the limestone arches. Closed doors along the corridor are dark brown, glossy under layers of shellac. Each has a brass plate in the middle, at eye level, showing a number. It feels remotely reminiscent of the Residential School, emptied of children on summer vacation.

Two further guards at the elevator helpfully provide instructions for proceeding, and carved brass numbers inside the cubicle light up silently in sequence. Sitting Wind hands a note to another uniformed guard at door number 410 and, as if awaiting his arrival, a person immediately emerges to lead him into the meeting.

To his delight several federal ministers are there, including Prime Minister Trudeau. These are precisely the people who can help me now, he realizes with smug delight. These are the bosses he needs to speak with.

The Land Claims Commissioner wanted to see him, it appears, in order to surprise him with an offer to settle a dispute over mineral rights to land received in trade when the Trans-Canada highway was widened. To that end, the commissioner hands him a draft letter, explaining that should Sitting Wind sign this letter when it is received at Calgary, the tribe will receive full title to eighteen thousand acres of land north of Morleyville.

Sitting Wind's response is spontaneous enthusiasm. He is momentarily unaware that this land is not new land, but merely the same land already traded, although held up by dispute.

"Thank you very much. I know we Stoneys can use all the land we can get, especially for more pasture." He shakes hands with them, pleased. Surely the council and the people back home can only applaud him when he returns with this surprise gift.

Indian Affairs Minister Jean Chretien motions to the chairman for the floor.

"I want to take this opportunity also to congratulate Chief Frank. I have seen your economic development plan, Frank, and I think you are to be commended for your progressive goals. There are excellent, workable ideas there which must be pursued. I want to encourage you to see them through, and my department will do everything possible to help. In fact, I have instructed department officials to sit down with you and your staff as soon as possible and develop your ideas into a five year plan that will fit the department's mandate. Once that is complete, we will be in a position to forward such funds as are required to carry out the plan."

Sitting Wind nods again enthusiastically. They like his plans for jobs and education: the Band cattle operation, the new sawmill, road and house construction, and tourism projects such as a commercial development at the Kananaskis intersection, which would include a tepee rental village, a handicraft store, restaurant, and a palisade area containing a dance circle and photography backdrop. A wilderness school has been proposed to council by one of the non-Stoney expert advisers, as has a co-op grocery store, and a ski hill on the south side of Chiniki Lake. How can he go wrong with all the support being offered at the highest levels? How can people back home even question his success when big-shots at the top are shaking his hand and promising that he can count completely on the government's support with money and advice: as much as is required? It is a big promise; but he believes them.

"Well Frank, it appears that you're the person we'll be dealing with," Prime Minister Trudeau says immediately after Chretien is finished. "Congratulations."

Sitting Wind turns to accept the praise. Trudeau casts his eyes mischievously about the table.

"The Honourable John Diefenbaker," he says, "became a chief such as you are; but unfortunately I myself have not yet been able to mimic his achievement. I guess I still lack the required age and wisdom." A rumble of laughter rolls around the circle.

"More seriously though," he continues, "it would appear that we will now be able to make even better progress with the Stoney Tribe. I understand that when there were several chiefs there was a recurring problem of approving an action with one of the bands, in that another's dissatisfaction would be incurred. I am confident, Chief Kaquitts, that this will change under your leadership.

Sitting Wind clears his throat to respond.

"Mr. Chairman," he begins, "I don't want to make any long speech or anything like that. But what I wanted to tell you is that there are quite a few people on the reserve spreading stories that I think are untrue. The reason is, I think, that they don't understand. Especially some of the elders, they are saying that the way we have changed to a one-chief system will go against the Treaty. They are worried that the Treaty will be less strong now. That's all I wanted to say; that maybe you would be able to sign a letter promising that the Treaty will not change."

They listen intently to Sitting Wind's request. Concerned. Chretien, quickly grasping the problem, reassures him with strong words that in no way can this affect the Treaty. He will have his secretary prepare a letter to that effect immediately.

"This letter with your signature right on it," Sitting Wind says later pumping Chretien's hands warmly at the exit, "this should straighten out any misunderstandings among my people back home."

"I hope so, Frank. And good luck." Chretien pats his shoulder in encouragement. "Call my office any time you need assistance."

Once inside the taxi, Sitting Wind withdraws the letter again from his jacket's inside pocket, and studies Chretien's sprawling signature. The people should be impressed. They must believe it. They must.

The firm bed in his hotel room appears inviting when he re-enters at the morning's end. It feels as if a full and exhausting day has just passed. He cannot erase Morley from his mind, the cynical sneers, the backbiters visiting one another like conspirators late at night. He cannot switch off images of the letter with the scrawled signature, the disarming banter of the government leaders in the meeting. How will people respond when he returns? What will they say?

His appetite fading, Sitting Wind orders up beer, switches on the TV and flips the channel selector until a lively wrestling match suddenly fills the screen. Sweet Daddy Siki's sweat gleams under camera lights. Voices clamoring from the dark perimeter beyond immediately attack. "Squeeze his head! His head! In the head! In de head. Indian head! Indian! We want the Indian! We want the Indian! We want the Indian! We want another chief! We want help! Somebody help! Kill him! Help!"

They are like people back home, overwhelming in their demands. Everyone wants help of some kind. How will he be able to satisfy them? Satisfy all of them? It sees impossible. Restlessly, he switches the TV off again, and stands before the window overlooking a paved parking lot.

Light snow has started to descend in swirls. A rusty wet dog hunches painfully against a concrete tire bumper, sniffs briefly toward its leavings, and becomes lost among the parked cars, only its four legs visible now and then as it moves beneath fenders and among tires.

The whiteman's government seems so different from that of the reserve. It seems that an Ottawa minister like Chretien can make any decision he desires and count on the fact that most people do not wish to be disturbed by the details of his decisions. He can hide behind the faceless numbers, and need not fear a few protestors. But the reserve is a small community, everyone related, like family. If someone disagrees with you on the reserve you cannot escape the name calling, the finger-pointing. You are made to feel as if you have personally hurt your own brother or sister.

Moving to the foot of the bed Sitting Wind begins to remove his sports jacket. Although desperately craving release from the tension crowding his mind, he suppresses the notion that staying in Ottawa a couple of extra days would be heavenly: a drunken, oblivious escape from it all.

He cannot escape, because they will be waiting for him back home. His supporters will wait for the good news he will bring them, especially now that he has met with the prime minister. And his opponents also will wait poised to cut down and savagely undermine his every attempt to hold the one-chief system together. Why are people more easily attracted to believing the destructive gossip than the constructive? It's almost as if they want to disbelieve the possibility of progress. Is it because the risks of change are greater with those who are desperate? That there is security in maintaining a known level of even desperate poverty? If there were only an answer.

When he allows his jacket to slip onto the bed, an unseen force suddenly takes command of his body. In an instant he is helplessly thrust forward, face down onto the mattress. Simultaneously, a loud sound rips through the room, like a jumbo jet passing within inches of his back. And wind. There is wind. The window is ajar, and something alive rushes out through its narrow four-inch gap.

It happens so quickly that he wonders whether the event is real or a spiritual vision. He tests his senses. Remaining motionless on the bed he listens, his ears at maximum alertness, his body tuned to every sensation that might follow. Suddenly an owl hovers over his head, hesitates. Then its claws clutch his skull, squeezing, and at the same time it flaps its wings more vigorously, as if attempting to carry him off. He is frozen in amazement, in this moment of terror, not knowing what may follow next.

Suddenly the owl is gone. He lies still, trying to regain the balance of his body's senses, assessing whether the sensation of crimped pain on his skull are real or imagined. Slowly he turns his face to the side, studying the window. But there is a screen. The owl could not have been an ordinary one. There is no way in or out of the room. Bringing his arm up slowly, he feels his scalp for blood. But there is none.

"Absolutely not," Mike Kartushyn insists vehemently. "I have checked with the regional director, and so far as we at Indian Affairs are concerned there are no legal grounds to declare the election null and void. I have sent you a letter in the mail to that effect."

"There are some people standing beside me now, with a large petition. Could be close to four hundred names," Sitting Wind replies uncertainly.

"I'll stand my ground on this, Frank. There has been a properly conducted, legal referendum and vote, and as far as we're concerned, it's final."

"Good." Sitting Wind hangs up the phone with dignity.

But it is not good. Under pressure from a hastily drawn up band members' petition, a majority of council has, in his absence, already signed a resolution reverting back to the old three-chief system. Although Indian Affairs refuses to recognize the petition, Band members are now trying to pressure Sitting Wind into signing it as well.

Will he go against the majority? Will he fight alongside Indian Affairs? Will he fight against his brothers and sisters?

The turmoil was whipped into a veritable storm during his two-day absence. "The reason the Minister so willingly signed the letter," the opponents immediately accused, "is that he knows he will trick us with this down the road. And you Frank Kaquitts, are helping him. That's what kind of a chief you are."

"Okay," one of the petitioners presses Sitting Wind. "You might as well stop fighting against your own people. You will find out later that we are right, that this was all a mistake. We know you don't wish to ruin the lives of future generations, so why don't you join us and sign this petition, as we have?"

Sitting Wind looks into the faces circling him. They are angry, scared. Behind the immediacy of the moment he senses the years, the decades of poverty, of suppression, of having a second-class, lower-class self-image ground into them like salt on sores. He cannot hurt them. He cannot hurt his own family even if their anger is directed at him. Never.

His fingers fondle his amulet, a sacred wind-polished pebble around his neck.

"I was at a sweat ceremony at the same moment," his sister-in-law said, starting in alarm when he related the hotel experience to his family. "I was instructed to be there but I didn't know why. Now I realize they were trying to kill you!" she cried.

She went on to explain how some of his opponents had hired strong medicine men from another reserve to conduct black magic against him, to try and kill him through medicine. Had they succeeded, he would have succumbed. The coroner's report would have simply stated, heart attack. The intervention of his guardian Wind Spirit saved him.

But what was being signalled to him by the Wind? Should he now give in, acknowledge the desperation of their panic? Could their fears be based on even a small element of truth? It would be reason enough.

Extending his hand, he receives the petition: scribbles of blue and black ink on lined paper. Page after page. His eyes scan the first few names — the elders'.

"We don't want to lose the Treaty. It's all that is left for our survival!" He recalls their hopeless arguments.

They hand him a pen. It is so hard to trust your future in the hands of whitemen, when in the past they have taken so much, so many times over again. The Treaty: like a small log to cling to in the middle of a lake.

Bow River near Morley
October, 1975

"You whitemen are starving us Indians. You have killed our wild game and now we have no food. This is why we have been on the warpath. And your redcoats and military are of no help to us!"

Sitting Wind manages to deliver the bitter criticisms in a more severe and dignified tone of voice, one which would have become Sitting Bull.

"That's good, just like that! Great stuff!" shouts the director. "Okay. Roll."

Composing a stone-cold face, Sitting Wind repeats his lines again at Paul Newman seated opposite him in the tepee. The actor is attired flamboyantly, arrogantly, to represent a romanticized Buffalo Bill: waved hair flowing, a neatly trimmed Colonel Sanders beard, a buckskin jacket alive with tassles, and white gauntlets which he has removed from his hands and is twisting smugly in his fists.

"My governors are offering a hand of friendship," Buffalo Bill replies evenly. "They desire to help our Indian brothers, and give you supplies for survival."

Sitting Bull would have considered this claim at length, responding carefully. What choices did he have?

For that matter what choices do today's Indian people have? Whitemen have occupied the land, game has slowly disappeared from the prairie and foothills and mountains, and where small pockets of game still remain they have become intensively managed; in short, Indians' traditional way of life is crippled, meaningless, stripped of its fundamental purpose.

What option remained but for Sitting Bull to accept an offer, any offer? There could have been only three choices, and two of them were virtually unthinkable: to attempt to kill every single whiteman who had come to take over the land, or to starve to death slowly as game populations dwindled to nothing. The third choice was to accept the whiteman's offer of help. Help in *his* way, in terms of the way *he* survives, help that would mean working for goods or money. Working. Jobs.

"If you have come to give us blankets," Sitting Wind responds with suitably measured pride, "and flour and tobacco, then we will stop fighting you. Because my people are cold without enough hides for clothes, and hungry without enough meat for food."

Paul Newman nods his head in concession, offering a handshake. And the cameraman pans right, simultaneously widening his lens angle to take in the entire tepee, and beyond the tepee the snow dusted flats extending to a wide bend in the Bow River. The scene could really have taken place in a remote portion of winter prairie in the upper Missouri somewhere, during the dead of winter. During the early eighteen hundreds.

The cameraman signals a stop, and the actors and stand-bys soon collapse in a babble of small talk. Sitting Wind tugs at his head-dress which has shifted slightly off center. Geraldine Chaplin, appearing from an informal melee behind the camera, offers him assistance. She plays the role of Annie Oakley, a hot-shot cowgirl. The half dozen or more white ermine skins falling down each side of his face nudge one another softly as she fluffs and aligns them with a flick of nimble fingers.

He is adorned with a heavy necklace of porcupine quills and elk incisors, and a plain buckskin shirt with fringes on the sleeves.

"That's better," she croons. "You look stunning! Simply stunning."

This new opportunity arrived last June. "We are searching for a Stoney to play as Sitting Bull in the movie *Buffalo Bill: Wild West Show*," the producer explained to Council. "He should be an older person who has a rather small build."

Immediately Sitting Wind knew he would be chosen. The part would fit him perfectly, and he had been on camera before: for interviews about his art work. He was experienced in acting and he understood art because of the Banff School of Fine Arts. Immediately, he had started growing his hair, and he now wears braids such as those worn in the old days. "A remarkable resemblance to Sitting Bull," the director beamed.

He was ready for a change. His mind was finally rid of its council-related turmoil. Once he signed the petition, his initiatives and enthusiasm were deflated, exploded into silent suffering and utter frustration. He had been negated. He had offered his generous help, but for his efforts he had become publicly and completely dishonoured, disclaimed, mortified.

He was too old to give reign to tears. He could not see himself cowering as a school child against white siding, basking in evening sun among the ground squirrels. Even Kathleen could stack no comfort against his pride. Recently, his thoughts reverted to a curious mixture of Christian love for those who are troubled and traditional unbending resolve never to bow to setbacks.

The other two former chiefs were quickly re-instated to finish their terms, and he finished his term as chief of the Chiniki Band. With help from Indian Affairs, he was able to obtain a loan to set up a Hannigan's restaurant outlet along the Trans-Canada. But even that fell through when the chain went bankrupt, and the Band was unable to recover invested money.

The truth in retrospect must be evident: all through his life his real interests have been in art and teaching and helping. Perhaps that's where he really belongs. Perhaps he has continuously misinterpreted his dreams, narrowly assuming he was destined to be a great leader. Perhaps there was a more cryptic meaning not yet discovered, a meaning more closely related to art and acting.

"Time for lunch," the director announces, and the various actors, camera technicians, lighting and sound assistants, all disperse to quarters hidden within the replica western village constructed in detail immediately adjacent to their tepee.

Every morning's breakfast at the set is followed by a meeting at which actors and workers are issued instruction about the day's shoot. Sitting Wind is eager to participate, and carefully hides his disquiet about how the Sitting Bull tale is being distorted. This is not how the serious story was told to him, handed down orally through generations. It seems the director's approach is not to present history as it really happened. He is merely fooling around, turning it into some sort of rock musical to make it more exciting.

Grandpa once told him the tale. "When my mother was a young girl," he said, "there was a great warrior named Sitting Bull. He was the most powerful Indian of his time. The mention of his name alone would conjure up respect and awe in people's thoughts, because his bravery in battle had become known far and wide.

"One day a Stoney medicine man proclaimed he had an important message relayed through a dream. Everyone listened attentively. He declared that Sitting Bull was on his way to visit the Stoney people and would arrive within a matter of days.

"Immediately the people became busy with preparations, and were excited, wondering how they should behave in the presence of such a powerful leader. They wondered among themselves what sort of a person he would turn out to be: probably a giant man who would inspire trembling in his enemies by merely staring them coldly in the eyes. Everyone eagerly awaited his visit to see him and to listen to his great words. All the people, including my mother's parents," Grandpa continued, "erected their tepees at the west end of Morley Flats, near where the Kananaskis and Bow Rivers meet. They camped there for two days before Sitting Bull arrived. He was visiting Indian bands all over the prairies and foothills at this time, deliberating with Chiefs about settlers, and dwindling game.

"On the third day the medicine man announced that Sitting Bull was now close at hand. So the Chief sent out a scout to investigate. The scout returned at mid-morning reporting that he was almost arrived. 'But his party consists of only five people,' the guide observed. 'And Sitting Bull appears to be a very small, unimposing man.'

"When he approached Morley Flats, emerging from trees to the south, the medicine man went to greet him and escort him into camp. They tied their horses and sat down with the leaders, Sitting Bull praying over the food. Being a Sioux, his language was similar to Stoney language. We could understand him easily. And he was not frightening or mean, but simple, plain, and kind.

"After their meal was finished, he stood up and explained to everyone that Indians south of the border were being treated wretchedly by American soldiers, and were fighting for their lands and for their very survival. He warned us to beware of what was taking place, and to be alert. Even the chiefs and councillors were awed by the great strength of Sitting Bull's determination, compared to his small physical size.

"After visiting for half a day he moved on, having received gifts ofdry-meat and pemmican. And we learned," Grandpa concluded, "it is not the size of a person, but the size of his heart and of his courage which makes him strong."

From time to time throughout his own years, Sitting Wind has reminded himself that no greater amount of courage is required in a person's life than that amount required to remain ordinary.

The thought seems to apply also to his current movie star associates. He really enjoys their company, and is amazed to discover they are ordinary people like himself. Other Stoneys loaf around the set daily. They wish to see Paul Newman; they come to stare at him. But Paul Newman laughs at them evasively, waves them aside saying, "Go and see Sitting Wind. He is a star."

The lunchroom is an Atco trailer, hidden behind a facade of vertical sawboards duplicating the front of a Texas general store. Today there are tuna sandwiches with lettuce and milk or coffee.

"So, what are your plans once the movie is finished?" Geraldine Chaplin asks cheerfully from her seat diagonally across the table, which is covered with pink checkered vinyl. She is a good actress, he believes. And she treats him as an equal, always in high spirits.

After the election, early last spring, he was appointed to the education committee with several other elders. The school welcomed him back as guidance counsellor assistant, to visit parents whose children are frequently absent from classes. "There is a bully at school who is always beating up my child," complained one mother. "The teachers simply don't care at all what happens to our little kids." Another explained she could afford no clothes or food for her children because her husband was always on the drunk and she did not receive enough support from welfare. Some say the roads are bad and wreck their cars: there should be buses.

Although council problems are not his worry anymore, school problems seem too ready to fill the vacuum. Why do people not take more initiative of their own to solve their problems? Must council members, teachers, guidance assistants and Indian Affairs representatives bear all their responsibilities?

No, this is not what he wants to be doing down the road.

"Well...." Sitting Wind begins to answer, still unsure about his alternatives. "If I could be a movie star for the rest of my life, that would be nice. Otherwise, I guess I should be painting. That's what I'm best at."

"You paint?" Geraldine lifts her eyes in surprise. Her lips are round and red. "You mean... like an artist with water colours or oils? Painting pictures and such?"

"Yup," Sitting Wind replies, his eyes lighting up. "Oils. I happen to be the best Indian artist around; possibly in all of Canada. I graduated from the Banff School of Fine Arts about fifteen years ago and have sold my paintings all over the world. I suppose, since you're from the States, you may not have heard of me before. But I'm pretty well known. Sitting Wind. That's my true name. Sitting Wind. Now that I think of it," he cannot resist a chuckle, "my name sounds a lot like Sitting Bull."

"Why, Frank!" she exclaims in amazement. "From Sitting Wind to Sitting Bull! You're a man of many talents. That's wonderful. I would like to see your paintings. Would you be able to show me some? Tell me you'll show me your work. I would love to see it for myself."

Sitting Wind recalls a similar invitation from Peter Whyte, years ago. It was the start of a new road.

"...Pete is a little better tonight, and has begun to drink orange juice and water again," Catharine wrote to Sitting Wind in late November, 1966. "If your friend could get some of that brew which he believes will help Pete, bring it up to Banff.... It is so hard to know what is best to do, but I have great faith in herbs and other natural things that you know about and have found successful over the years."

"The trouble," he explains apologetically to Geraldine, "is that I haven't been painting too much lately because I've been too busy with Council and all that.... But I taught kids in the Morley school for seven years."

"That's terrific! You should keep it up, because I'll bet you're damned good at it."

"I guess I should be starting it again. You could be right. It's hard to know who to listen to, which is often my problem. I prefer to please people."

The two fall to eating in silence for a moment, the floor resounding hollowly under the heavy shuffling of others entering and finding their sandwiches and donuts. Over the edge of his sandwich Sitting Wind glances in her direction and finds her adding sugar to her coffee and stirring it round and round. It is hot for her lips, and her eyes crimp in an attempt to sip a small amount.

"Do you know I had a vision once?" he says tentatively, as if possibly risking too much. "I had a vision that I was walking with Jesus Christ."

Geraldine's mouth stops chewing and her eyes draw up, her sandwich sliding down to the plate before her.

"Jesus Christ?" she inquires, studying his expression.

"I know you may not believe me, but it's true. I have had visions and dreams before, warning me I am going to be a leader."

"I believe you." She says it seriously, slowly. Her eyes are staring at him from centuries away.

"It happened about ten years ago," Sitting Wind continues. "When I was working for Poole Construction. My friend, George Labelle, was working with me. We were building the spillway down Whiteman's Pass near Canmore, and the foreman had us working eight hours a day standing in icy mountain water with hip waders, cleaning out rocks. Even though the sun was hot outside we were always cold. Our families were camped in tepees at Indian Flats across the river.

"Anyway, after two weeks I came down sick, maybe with pneumonia. So my family picked me up and drove me to the Morley Hospital. When I arrived a nurse took my temperature, but she said it was normal. There was nothing wrong with me.

"I knew she was mistaken, because I was aching all through my body. So back at our car we agreed the nurse had taken my temperature too hastily. She did not wait long enough for my body to adjust to the temperature inside the hospital, especially since I had been standing so long in cold water. So I re-entered, and explained this to her. She then waited five minutes before taking my temperature again. When she read the thermometer this time, she suddenly exclaimed 'Oh, my God!' and ran to summon a doctor by phone.

"Immediately she put me to bed. The doctor instructed her to give me medicine. I think she gave me a couple of inches of whiskey, and pills: but I don't know what kind they were. Then they left me there, alone. When a meal was brought to my bed, I didn't eat it because I wasn't hungry.

"Perhaps this vision came while I was awake after midnight or during very early morning hours. All of a sudden I felt as if a blind was brought over my face. A hand appeared in front of me and pointed to the east telling me to look there. Obediently, I looked eastward and saw a light. It was bright, so bright I couldn't stare at it directly. It drew closer and closer, and then stopped in front of the hospital, right in front of me.

"Then a person appeared beside me, standing; he seemed to be covered with a large plastic bag. When I saw him I wondered, Who could this be? This must be a joke or something. But then the hand appeared again and told me this person is Jesus Christ.

"Immediately, I wondered why he would wish to see me. But before I could speak, he said to me, 'You are going to travel with me.' He said, 'We are departing right now; we shall go up the hill to the Morley Trading Post store.' So he led me outside, and we started walking side by side up the hill.

"About half way up this hill we met a young Stoney hurrying down in the opposite direction. When he drew close, I called to him and said, 'Hey! Wait a minute! This is Jesus Christ!' He thought I was crazy and ran quickly on. His response disappointed me; I thought, here I am going up the highway with Jesus Christ, and no one seems to understand.

"We continued up the hill and met another fellow at the summit. I stopped him and said, 'Hey! This is Jesus Christ! Don't you wish to shake hands with him?' He said to me, 'You must be kidding, there's nothing beside you! I'll see you later.' He also passed on.

"Shortly before arriving at the Trading Post turnoff, we met my friend George Labelle. George was in a good mood, not drunk but jolly. I stopped him and introduced my companion, 'This is Jesus Christ. Don't you wish to shake hands with him?' He looked at me and replied, 'I don't see anyone here other than yourself!' But he held out his hand for the humour of it. The hand of Jesus Christ grabbed his hand and shook it. His hair stood on end, and mine too. Wow, I thought to myself, this is truly a miracle.

"Then suddenly I was back in my hospital bed, and the hand appeared in front of me again. The hand told me, 'You are now going to travel with Jesus Christ, starting from here and right around the world,' and while saying so, he brought his finger in a semi circle fully around the bottom of the globe. He continued, 'You are going to be all right, you need worry about nothing. This does not mean you are going to die.'

That was how my vision ended." Sitting Wind's eyes skip across Geraldine's face. "Although I'm not too sure what I'll be doing next, that's one of the ways by which I've been told that there is something important for me to do in my life, and that I have nothing to fear when the going gets rough."

The actress seems uncertain how to respond. Frank is genuine. Utterly honest. He believes it completely.

"The funny part of it came right after that," Sitting Wind chuckles. "That was when it was barely light and I heard the nurses talking behind my door. One of them whispered to the other in low tones, 'What did the doctor order?' I couldn't understand all they said because they were speaking quietly. Then I heard the other reply. 'Who's going to do the dirty work?' When I heard this I assumed they meant they were going to give me a needle to kill me.

"So I waited until they were busy eating downstairs at noon hour, and then searched for my clothes in an office, put them on, and escaped by the front door. I walked up the road, up the same hill of my vision, toward the highway to hitch a ride. Fred Holloway was at the Trading Post and gave me a ride to Banff Indian Days where I stayed with my uncle, Walking Buffalo."

Sitting Wind pauses for a breath and bites into his second sandwich. The white bread is sweet and spongy. Geraldine is eying him with genuine sympathy.

"I think it's wonderful that you have visions to guide you and to make you stronger," she says thoughtfully. "I wish I could remember my dreams. Maybe I never dream, or perhaps only rarely." Suddenly she giggles almost girlishly. "God knows, I definitely could benefit from a little divine guidance now and then."

"It seems it's easier for us Indians to have special contact with

Spirits. I have dreams, too. You don't have dreams?''

The actress admits that she rarely if ever dreams. If she does she cannot recall them. ''Nor visions either. I'm not sure I would know what a vision is should I ever be so lucky to experience one,'' she chuckles. ''I take it they differ from dreams?''

''Yup. Visions are different,'' Sitting Wind instructs. ''You can tell when it is a vision because it happens right out of the blue, any time of day. You could even be busy doing something and suddenly you have a vision. Dreams come slowly, when you fall asleep or are in a trance. In fact, I had a dream right after this vision, when I was at Banff Indian....''

''Why don't we walk along the river,'' she cuts in. ''You could tell me as we walk. This room is intolerably stuffy when it fills up during meals.''

Sitting Wind obliges and they step down to soiled snow, buttoning their coats. A gusty dry wind has started from the west, a Chinook. Sitting Wind's eyes survey the sky over the mountains, lateral ribbons of plasticene cloud. The snow will be drifting by tonight.

''Now tell me your dream,'' she encourages.

''When I arrived at our Indian Days grounds,'' Sitting Wind continues, ''I told my uncle I had been feeling ill and needed a warm place to sleep. He suggested I stay and sleep in his tepee, under one of his buffalo robes. They are the warmest. Walking Buffalo prepared a medicine brew to warm me, as well as tea and pemmican. After I had wrapped myself into the buffalo robe and became warm with sleep, I began to dream.

''A small being approached me, and I recognized it as a dwarf — one of the little-people. First he offered me jewelry which I refused. I took nothing. The only thing I finally accepted was a little box containing an assortment of screws, nuts, nails and things.

''The dwarf who offered me these things came closer and smiled at me. He then offered me two large six foot snakes in a box. When I refused them, he shut the box and turned around, and suddenly I saw him transformed into a large snake.

''He came back as a dwarf and offered me another box which I also refused. When he turned around again he was suddenly transformed to a willow bush.

''Lastly he offered me a house, a beautiful log mansion. He led me through its many rooms. and while inside I peered through a window and saw many helpless and neglected people as my subjects, to rule over them like a dictator in whatever way I fancied. But I felt sorry for them. I didn't wish to rule them that way. So I refused his offer. Then everything vanished, except for a string of additional tiny little-people scrambling up the teepee pole and jumping off the end outside, above the smoke chute.''

Heavy boots crunching through crusts of old snow, the actors proceed silently toward the river. Sitting Wind cinches the zipper of his down jacket more closely to his chin as they come to a halt, where the gravel flat falls away into the river's gorge. The irregular breeze from the west is increasing in strength. Black water gleams coldly, slips along under pans of silvered ice.

''So do you think you will ever be chief again?'' Geraldine finally asks.

But he avoids the question; points out to her where they used to ford the river, summer and winter, before the bridge was built at Morley.

ℳorley

Summer, 1987

"*Aday! Aday! Weseejew!*" (Dad! Dad! A whiteman!)
The barefoot two year old pivots and retreats, half waddles back into a hallway beyond the kitchen, rounded belly wrapped snugly in a fresh Pamper. The bearded visitor is left waiting beyond the outside door, which is slightly ajar, his briefcase propped under one arm and a cassette recorder, wrapped in a mess of cord, suspended from the other.

A faint but penetrating odour of Pinesol enters his nostrils. Through the door's crack he observes that the vinyl kitchen floor has been recently cleaned and mopped, three stuffed plastic bags of garbage stacked against the wall, ready for pickup by the Morley Sanitation truck which is due to make its weekly stop. A kitchen table and four chairs are made of chromed tubing, vinyl seats. No effort has been made to hide the wear effected by the seventeen people living in this five-bedroom house.

Beyond the kitchen, two beds are visible in a living room, and lumpy bedding on the chesterfield suggests that someone is still wrapped within, although it is ten o'clock and images of Romper Room flash across a TV screen. The child, returning inquisitively behind Sitting Wind, is eating from a bag of Cheesies.

"Morning, Frank!" the visitor says cheerfully.

"Oh, Peter! Come on in! In fact, I'm ready. We can go right downstairs where it will be quiet."

The women will be busy upstairs, he explains, preparing breakfast, cleaning up; the kids running about, playing.

Sitting Wind leads his visitor down wooden stairs into the mouth of a dingy basement. Several scrawny kittens scurry from dark crevices behind a stack of half a dozen or more old mattresses. Elements of a hockey outfit and several uncased cassettes lay strewn about the cold concrete floor. Since laundry is taken to a laundromat in Canmore or Cochrane, there is no evidence of tubs and machines.

Proceeding approximately in the direction of a rumbling furnace,

Sitting Wind withdraws a key from his clothes and fits it to a padlock on a door.

As eyes adjust to dim light, black letters on a eroded yellow sign fixed over the door become visible: "Private. Indian Reserve." He found it along the gravel road once, near the Kananaskis highway. "I'm sort of a packrat, as you can see," he explains as he enters his sanctuary. "This is my place."

In the less than half-light, Peter eyes him with deliberate curiosity demanding further explanation.

"Of course, the whole house is my place," Sitting Wind laughs. "But, this here is *really* my place, if you know what I mean." The door opens, and he switches on a naked light bulb.

The walls of a roughly constructed eight by twelve room are encumbered with layers of relics, tools, mementos, and yellowed newspaper clippings. There must be tables and benches, but their tops are submerged under heaps of artifacts. Straining to comprehend its parameters of organization, Peter studies the room and its contents methodically. It is reminiscent of Calgary's Eighth Avenue second hand shops. An electric grindstone fixed to a narrow bench is linked to Sitting Wind's interest in crafts. So also are the shelves against a far wall, littered with bluestone carvings, ceremonial pipes in various stages of completion, peeled and carved sticks, spears, bows and arrows, beaded necklaces. A red vinyl chair, disgorging its seat stuffing, is located in a tight corner below a yellowed clipping:"Walking Buffalo Preaches Moral Rearmament." Among other glassware on the floor, still within easy reach, is a recently-empty whisky bottle wrapped in its original brown bag.

Toward the rear, another door leads into a second nine-by-nine room: a painting studio of sorts, also lit by a bare bulb, dominated by a rough hewn waist-high counter along one wall, bearing upright paintings of dark, earthy colours. The paintings are of mixed sizes, most just canvases, but some in dusty frames. A couple of jars contain brushes, although the solvents have long evaporated. And there are neglected tubes of oil paint.

"What it the purpose of this room, Frank?" Peter asks.

"This is where I do most of my painting. My studio, sort of."

"Have you been doing any painting lately?"

"Well, not too much. As soon as I clean it up a little then I'm going to start again. Get ready for the Olympics which are coming here next year. But I'm still kind of sick," he explains. "That's what is holding me up. The doctor said it would take me about three years to recover from the operation. I get tired pretty quick and then I need to lie down and rest.''

Peter pulls up a second chair and locates, among abandoned boots, an electrical socket to operate the tape recorder he squeezes onto the bench. The routine has become familiar to both. Once a week, until the story is complete. Sitting Wind, in preparation, is rummaging around, head bent to the floor. He finds what he is looking for, a small can to serve as spittoon. He enjoys a good chew during the recording sessions.

''Now what I would like you to do today, Frank,'' Peter begins once the recorder is switched on, ''is to describe how you see yourself, your family and Stoneys in general, as remaining different from the white society living around you. Tell me your thoughts about what has changed over the years, and about what differences persist.''

Sitting Wind considers the request before responding. It is a large topic.

''Well, to begin with, the way our household is organized is a lot different from that of whitemen's families. White people seem to know how to save. We don't seem to know that, because our parents taught us to share everything. White people for example, may give their kids an allowance, say twenty-five cents a day, for good behaviour and to teach them that this is a reward. But they don't let them spend it, they make them save it in a bank. We never seem to do that. First of all, we don't think of money as a way of teaching something. And when we do share some money with our kids we consider it for spending, for them to buy candy or whatever.

''I remember I used to get a quarter or fifty cents from my grandparents once in a while, but of course it didn't mean anything unless there was a store close by for candy or ice cream. When I was young in the bush we didn't need much money; we had everything.

''We were brought up more to share; not to be selfish. I think this must be the reason we don't know how to save. Even today I don't know how to save. As soon as we receive money it gets spent right away. The difficult part for us is planning for family expenses.

''Tell me more about how your household is organized,'' Peter says.

''We all live on my land here. This is the land our family has been on ever since I moved here, and all my family lives here. I guess you could say it's sort of like a camp in the old days. My oldest son and his wife have five children, but they have their own house behind the corral. My second son also lives with his wife in their own place; they're in a trailer beside here. But my wife Kathleen and our daughters with their kids all live in this house. We are now three generations living upstairs in this house, because there are no houses available for my daughters and their children. My daughters' husbands are having too much of a hard time on their own, so my daughters don't wish to live with them.

"The way we work our meals in the household is that each mother and her children is treated as sort of a separate group and has her own cupboard for groceries. At the end of the day, if someone makes a meal she invites the other mothers, if they are home, to share the food being prepared. Usually they do, and in return offer to help, contributing some of their groceries as well. However, if the offered food is not to their liking, they may choose to wait and prepare their own dish once the first one is done with the kitchen.

"In the morning," Sitting Wind continues without breaking his measured and logical pace, "everyone is on his own in the family, as far as breakfast is concerned. Right now my wife and oldest daughter have to be out before nine for work at the Handicraft Store, so I woke them at seven, since I'm usually the first one up at five or six o'clock. I learned to get up early in the army. Before the army I would sleep all day if I could get away with it; but in the army they teach you discipline.

"They fix their own breakfasts, and mine as well. This morning I had Bran Flakes, that's what I prefer. Yesterday I had sardines from a can for lunch, although sometimes I cook a hamburger. At the end of the day the women return from their jobs, and they cook a big meal. Yesterday we had boiled moose ribs with potatoes with some Kraft macaroni and cheese. I usually like tea. The ribs were given to us by the family of the husband of one of my daughters.

"Before, while I was chief, groceries would be purchased with my money, but now I have only my pension and that's not enough for groceries. That's why Kathleen and Karen work at the handicraft shop. I guess we should do it like the whitemen; put all our money into one big pot and plan our expenditures together. But that is not the way we were brought up, not the way we're used to it. It would be a big change for us to do it like whitemen. The staple food items like potatoes and milk, items which everyone uses, we keep them together in the fridge.

"If we would know how to save and buy groceries as whitemen do, it would be better. It seems to me that white people know what to buy. The first thing some of us buy is pop and sweets.

"I am the boss in the house as far as authority is concerned. I try to make my grandchildren understand that they are not really in their own home, and therefore they have to respect this house, cause no damage. If I am watching TV, I teach them not to run and yell, but sit quietly and watch with me. My daughters don't mind if I discipline their kids. I also teach the kids that this is not a pig-pen. The house should be kept clean. This is the way I like to see them learn.''

As Sitting Wind takes a momentary spitoon break, Peter interrupts.

''I would like to ask you something more personal, Frank. A question dealing with your true feelings about various setbacks in your life.''

''Ask me anything!'' He responds with good humour. ''I've got nothing to hide.''

''Okay. It seems to me that throughout life your dreams have been frustrated time and time again. How are you coping with these frustrations? *Are* you coping? Are you drinking a little now and then, to escape them?''

''Drinking is not a problem, really,'' is his immediate reply. ''I can take it or leave it any time I choose.... But for the rest, I try not to think too much about the past. I am happy now to be with my wife and my children and grandchildren, and I like to paint and make crafts now and then. This way I have no worries.''

''Frank,'' Peter prods cautiously. ''I don't understand what goes on in a person's mind when he craves drink. These interviews, this story is about your life. The way it really was, and where it has led you. The way it is now. I don't see how we can leave this out.''

Sitting Wind hesitates, dodges. His hair is silk, silver. The braids falling to his chest are not as neat as they were yesterday when he rewound them. The wrinkles and scars on his face have deepened with age. He relaxes his hands in his lap.

''When I start drinking, it is because I fear failure.'' His voice is suddenly resigned, subdued. ''When I drink, it's because it seems that everything I tried during my life ended up in failure, even though I fought hard to set things right, to please people. I have become afraid of failure. Now I have become afraid even to try anything new. Afraid to dream.

''In the past, as I already told you, I have had a lot of dreams and visions telling me that I was supposed to become a leader. It was even predicted by Mountain Walker, when I received my sacred name. I have asked myself over and over again throughout my life, why me? I guess I must be a born leader. That's the only answer I can come up with.

''Repeatedly, I had the feeling that people wanted me to help them; but several times I tried. As soon as I did they threw me out. Thus I learned that people don't always want to listen to you. Rumours are bad this way; people seem to accept negative stories more readily than those that are positive, true. People are jealous easily. They feel that they don't want the other person to be successful, to get ahead.

"I was told from the beginning that the Wind would heal me and help me any time. But, I guess I should have paid more attention to the power of Wind. I was branded with this power, and I have neglected to use Wind as my brother. I have forgotten the real me too much. I have never yet used the power of the wind, ever in my life.

"The problem is that I still lack my power song, or chant. When I received my name the medicine man, Mountain Walker, gave me a song to use as my chant, but I was too small to remember it. And, although I was told through a vision that I would be informed of my song at the appropriate time, I am still waiting.

"My last hope is that my song will come soon. I have been told by the old people that you don't do things that you are not ordered to do; you must wait patiently. They assure me the Spirits will come. I could use other chants, but they won't be as strong, as effective. When I get my own true chant I will be able to do whatever I want to do. This is my last hope.

"But getting back to your first question." Sitting Wind changes the subject with determination. "There is a lot of difference between the way it was, and the way it is now.

"Take food for example. We are in the modern way of life now: plastic, sugar, pills. There is hardly anything pure to eat anymore. You buy meat in the store, it comes from a cow that has had all sort of medicines put into it before it was slaughtered. Even the blood is still in there. Even in the Residential School it was better than what we have today, because there was no medicine for cows then.

"The best food of all was the pure food we used to gather in the wilderness. Nothing was required to be bought then. I was originally taught the pure way, the best way. I guess it's sort of sad to me that from the old pure way we seem to have changed to.... How do you say that word? I just had that one word in mind which means you know everything and can do anything you wish.... 'Civilized.' That's it. Civilized is something I still don't completely understand. On the one hand we're supposed to be civilized now, but on the other it seems we're not there yet.

"Anyway, my life is not over by a long shot." He laughs gently. "So I still have a chance."

Frank Kaquitts' Family Tree

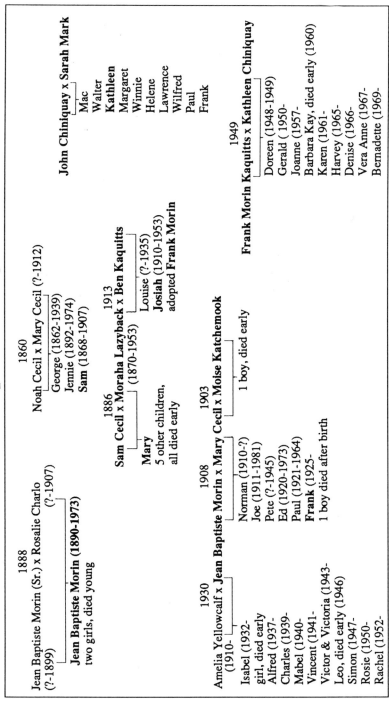

John Chiniquay x Sarah Mark

Mac
Walter
Kathleen
Margaret
Winnie
Helene
Lawrence
Wilfred
Paul
Frank

1949
Frank Morin Kaquitts x Kathleen Chiniquay

Doreen (1948-1949)
Gerald (1950-
Joanne (1957-
Barbara Kay, died early (1960)
Karen (1961-
Harvey (1965-
Denise (1966-
Vera Anne (1967-
Bernadette (1969-

1860
Noah Cecil x Mary Cecil (?-1912)

George (1862-1939)
Jennie (1892-1974)
Sam (1868-1907)

1913
Sam Cecil x Moraha Lazyback x Ben Kaquitts
(1870-1953)

Louise (?-1935)
Josiah (1910-1953)
adopted **Frank Morin**

Mary
5 other children,
all died early

1903
Mary Cecil x Moise Katchemook

1 boy, died early

1888
Jean Baptiste Morin (Sr.) x Rosalie Charlo
(?-1899)   (?-1907)

Jean Baptiste Morin (1890-1973)
two girls, died young

1908
Jean Baptiste Morin x Mary Cecil

Norman (1910-?)
Joe (1911-1981)
Pete (?-1945)
Ed (1920-1973)
Paul (1921-1964)
Frank (1925-
1 boy died after birth

1930
Amelia Yellowcalf x **Jean Baptiste Morin**
(1910-

Isabel (1932-
girl, died early
Alfred (1937-
Charles (1939-
Mabel (1940-
Vincent (1941-
Victor & Victoria (1943-
Leo, died early (1946)
Simon (1947-
Rosie (1950-
Rachel (1952-

Photo Credits

A Note About the Author

Peter Jonker, who has degrees in both English literature and in Recreation and Wildlife, has maintained a life-long interest in wilderness travel, Indian ways of living, and the dynamics of culture clash. He has worked with the Stoney Indians since 1976, and he lived on the Reserve at Morley for three years. An environmental consultant, playwright, photographer and writer, he currently lives in Canmore, Alberta.